2003

P9-ARF-211

Section 504 in the Classroom

Section 504 in the Classroom

How To Design and Implement Accommodation Plans

Lynda Miller
and
Chris Newbill

pro·ed
An International Publisher
8700 Shoal Creek Boulevard
Austin, Texas 78757-6897
800/897-3202 Fax 800/397-7633
Order online at http://www.proedinc.com

UNIVERSITY OF ST. FRANCIS
LIBRARY
JOLIET, ILLINOIS

© 1998 by PRO-ED, Inc.
8700 Shoal Creek Boulevard
Austin, Texas 78757-6897
800/897-3202 Fax 800/397-7633
Order online at http://www.proedinc.com

All rights reserved. No part of the material protected by this
copyright notice may be reproduced or used in any form or by
any means, electronic or mechanical, including photocopying,
recording, or by any information storage and retrieval system,
without the prior written permission of the copyright owner.

Library of Congress Cataloging-in-Publication Data

Miller, Lynda.
    Section 504 in the classroom : how to design and implement
  accommodation plans / Lynda Miller, Chris Newbill.
        p.   cm.
    Includes bibliographical references (p.   ) and index.
    ISBN 0-89079-748-X (alk. paper)
      1. Inclusive education—United States—Planning.   2. Handicapped—
    Education—United States—Planning.   3. Discrimination against the
    handicapped—United States—Prevention.   I. Newbill, Chris.
    II. Title.
LC1201.M55   1998
371.9′046—dc21   97-35305
                                                                      CIP

This book is designed in Goudy and Avant Garde.

Printed in the United States of America

    5   6   7   8   9   10   02

371.9046
M6492

354.51

Pub.

3-26-03

Contents

Preface

This book represents another in a series of books, articles, workshops, and school-based projects the two of us have collaborated on over the past 15 years. Our work together stems from our shared beliefs regarding learners, teaching, and educational policies and practices. Stated in its most basic form, our philosophy rests on the concept of educational care. What we mean by educational care can best be described as the thoughtful support of learners by teachers who believe that everyone is smart and capable and that teaching begins with finding out *how* students are smart.

In our experience people—regardless of age—learn what is important to them, and they pay attention to what they find interesting. It is not surprising, then, that students respect and learn from teachers who make the effort to discover what is important to their students and what they find interesting—in short, teachers who care about their students. Seen in this way, real learning can be said to originate and flourish in the context of the relationships established by teachers committed to the idea that their students' perspectives provide what no curriculum or test score can possibly offer. Educational caring originates in this commitment.

A major component of our philosophy of educational care is the idea that teaching works best when it focuses on students' strengths, rather than on what is wrong, disordered, or different from "normal." In fact, we question the idea that "normal" represents a real entity; we suggest that using the term to refer to school performance or achievement is a form of linguistic slippage resulting from a sloppy interpretation of the statistical concept of "average." Our belief, based on the concept of educational care, is that every student possesses learning strengths. Our job as teachers is to find out what those strengths are so we can capitalize on them in hooking our students' minds and hearts on the learning process.

Another aspect of the philosophy of educational care relates to difference. Our experience has shown us that all students, not just those identified as having "special needs," have unique talents as well as unique needs. What this means for us is that when we realize that diversity includes everyone, classrooms can be truly inclusive learning environments. In this view, inclusion does not represent something new or different from what constitutes good teaching. Rather, inclusion offers a means for providing caring, individualized instruction to *every* student.

We undertook writing this book about Section 504 because we, like many of our teaching colleagues, had not realized the possibilities 504 offers. As we began designing accommodations and modifications for students under Section 504 plans, we realized that the process constitutes a means for improving our teaching, our relationships with our students, the communication we have with our colleagues, and the quality and frequency of contacts we have with our students' families. We have written this book for those of you interested in addressing these same issues in your own work.

Our goal in this book is to invite you to consider Section 504 as a way to move beyond mere compliance—following the rules—and into the realm of truly caring educational practice. In our attempt to convey the philosophy outlined above, we have included throughout the book excerpts describing students for whom we have developed Section 504 plans, and we have shown you the plans themselves so you can share with us, at least vicariously, the process of designing educational plans based on students' strengths and needs.

We should also tell you what we have *not* included in the book. Though we have addressed some of the legal aspects of Section 504, we have not delved deeply into legality issues. We refer you to a companion book, *Section 504 and Public Schools: A Resource Guide for Determining Eligibility and Developing Accommodation Plans*, by Tom Smith and James R. Patton (1998). Smith and Patton's book takes you through Section 504 from the legal standpoint, including an analysis of the statute and its definitions, the eligibility determination and accommodation plan processes, and due process under the statute. The authors describe pertinent legal cases to date and include a section on frequently asked questions.

We hope reading our book offers you the opportunity to examine your own beliefs and ideas about what constitutes good teaching. And we hope learning about Section 504 will provide you, as it has us, with another means for furthering the philosophy of educational care. Enjoy!

Acknowledgments

From Chris: To Lynda, thank you for your friendship, your humor and insight, and all the times you've invited me to play. Thanks also to Rosemary Stevenson for the wonderful educational care she has given my children.

From Lynda: My sincere thanks to Jim Patton for his guidance and thoughtfulness as we brought this book from an idea to a reality. A giant thank-you to Lynn C. Miller, whose collegiality and mentoring supported me throughout the writing process. And to Chris, without whom this book would not have come into existence. Thank you for your commitment and dedication to education and for sharing your wisdom.

Introduction to Section 504

Chapter 1

Background

Section 504 of the Rehabilitation Act of 1973 is part of the larger rehabilitation act passed by Congress to ensure two broad categories of support for individuals with disablities: first, that individuals with disabilities are provided a free and appropriate education (FAPE), and, second, that individuals with disabilities are accommodated and employed without discrimination related to their disabilities.

Section 504 languished for over two decades in the shadow of the Eduucation for All Handicapped Children Act of 1975 (P.L. 94-142) and its recent reauthorization as the Individuals with Disabilities Education Act of 1990 (IDEA). P.L. 94-142 provided and IDEA currently provides, through the U.S. Department of Education, federal mandates and funding to ensure a free and appropriate education for individuals with disabilities. Section 504, on the other hand, falls under the responsibility of the Office for Civil Rights (OCR), which for many years focused on the area of employment for individuals with disabilities and individuals who are members of minorities.

More recently, however, the OCR has become proactive in its enforcement of Section 504 in the field of education of individuals with disabilities. (OCR is still active in enforcing Section 504 in the area of employment; in this book, however, we focus exclusively on the educational aspects of 504). In addition, according to the Council of Administrators of Special Education (CASE), advocacy groups and the legal system have "increasingly focused on Section 504's requirements regarding the responsibilities of schools and school districts to provide special accommodations and services for students with special needs to participate in and benefit from public education programs and services" (Council for Administrators of Special Education, 1992, p. 1).

As CASE points out, Section 504 prohibits discrimination against persons with disabilities (both students and staff members) by school districts receiving federal assistance of any kind for any program or activity. What this means is that districts may not discriminate against any person with a disability, regardless of whether the program or activity in which that person is involved receives federal funding directly.

Most public schools, educational cooperatives, regional education units, and state departments of education receive substantial federal funding. According to Street and Smith (1996), examples of such programs include

- school lunch programs;
- special education (IDEA) programs;
- transportation grants;
- remedial programs; and
- gifted education programs.

Most educators are familiar with IDEA. Few, however, are as familiar with Section 504: what the law says, district responsibilities, classroom requirements, the effects on teachers, and the ramifications for students and their families. In this book we have collected a set of resources for educators to use in designing, implementing, and evaluating Section 504 plans for students with disabilities.

Drawing from our experiences with Section 504, we have included in later sections a description of Section 504 and its definitions, a comparison of Section 504 and IDEA, descriptions of the processes we use to identify, evaluate, and provide appropriate services to students, and discussion of the procedural guidelines we have found to work in conjunction with developing Section 504 plans. In later chapters we discuss the types of modifications we use in 504 plans; show you the actual forms that we and others have developed for the various aspects of developing, implementing, and evaluating Section 504 plans; and share a variety of stories describing our efforts with students, their families, and their teachers.

What Is Section 504?

Section 504 is a broad civil rights law protecting the rights of individuals in programs and activities that receive federal funding from the U.S. Department of Education. The law protects all school-age children who qualify as "handicapped" according to the definitions described below. In addition, we refer you to the Glossary, which includes definitions of terms associated with Section 504. Section 504 of the Rehabilitation Act of 1973 states: "No otherwise qualified individual with handicaps in the United States shall, solely by reason of her or his handicap, as defined in section 706(8) of this title, be excluded from the participation in, be denied the benefits of, or be subjected to discrimination under any program or activity receiving Federal financial assistance or under any program or activity conducted by any Executive agency or by the United States Postal Service" (Sec. 794).

The act provides a set of definitions that explicate exactly what is meant by "individual with a handicap," as well as defining the impact of the handicap or condition on a "major life activity." Thus, an individual with a handicap is defined as any individual who

(i) has a physical or mental impairment which substantially limits one or more of such person's major life activities,

(ii) has a record of such impairment, or

(iii) is regarded as having such an impairment. (Sec. 706.(8))

Further, physical or mental impairment is described as

(A) any physiological disorder or condition, cosmetic disfigurement, or anatomical loss affecting one or more of the following body systems: neurological; musculoskeletal; special sense organs; respiratory, including speech organs; cardiovascular; reproductive; digestive; genito-urinary; hermic and lymphatic; skin; and endocrine; or

(B) any mental or psychological disorder, such as mental retardation, organic brain syndrome, emotional or mental illness, and specific learning disabilities. (34 Code of Federal Regulations Part 104.3)

Major life activities are defined as "functions such as caring for one's self, performing manual tasks, walking, seeing, hearing, speaking, breathing, learning and working" (34 Code of Federal Regulations Part 104.3). Having a record of such an impairment means "has a history of, or has been classified as having, a mental or physical impairment that substantially limits one or more major life activities" (34 Code of Federal Regulations Part 104.3). Finally, one who is regarded as having an impairment is defined as one who

(A) has a physical or mental impairment that does not substantially limit major life activities but is treated by a recipient as constituting such a limitation;

(B) has a physical or mental impairment that substantially limits major life activities only as a result of the attitudes of others toward such impairment; or

(C) has none of the impairments defined but is treated by a recipient as having such an impairment" (34 Code of Federal Regulations Part 104.3).

In delineating who is qualified for Section 504 protection, the statute refers to students who meet the definitions above; those who have a physical or mental impairment *significantly* affecting a major life activity qualify, even if these students do not fall within the special education categories of individuals with disabilities—which would qualify them for special education services.

What Disabilities Are Covered Under Section 504?

The definitions provided in Section 504 specify that students are protected if they have, have had, or are regarded as having a physical or mental impairment. In our experience, most educators have little difficulty understanding that a physical disability or impairment can affect major life activities, including learning. Most teachers, for instance, see clearly why a student returning to school from a concussion might need accommodations such as a reduced school day, reduced homework assignments, or rest breaks in the nurse's office throughout the day for a period of several weeks.

However, some teachers experience more difficulty understanding how mental impairments might affect learning to the extent that students might require modifications or accommodations to support their learning needs. We have encountered a teacher who, when informed that one of her students had been diagnosed as having Attention-Deficit/Hyperactivity Disorder (ADHD) and that a Section 504 planning meeting was scheduled to design an accommodation plan, responded with, "Oh, she doesn't need special help. She just needs to learn to sit still and pay attention. Besides, I don't believe she has ADHD." This teacher's response illustrates, albeit to the extreme, the attitude that mental impairments are really just a matter of character or willpower, and that if students would learn to pay attention, or learn to sit still, or learn to get along better, or learn to organize better, they would learn just fine. Such an attitude indicates an absence of understanding of how mental conditions or impairments can—and do—affect our ability to participate in the instructional process, especially if that process is geared to the "norm" or to the "good" student, whose learning needs fit precisely with the methods used by the teacher to deliver instruction.

The following list is a sampler of the types of physical and mental conditions and impairments covered under Section 504. The list makes clear that Section 504 covers a wide array of conditions and handicaps. And keep in mind, as we will discuss below, that Section 504 covers *all* students with handicaps, regardless of whether they qualify for services under IDEA, which receives additional federal funding.

Examples of Handicapping Conditions Under Section 504

ADD/ADHD

anorexia

asthma

behavioral difficulties

bulimia

cerebral palsy

communicable diseases

conduct disorder

depression

drug/alcohol addiction (if student is no longer using drugs; if using alcohol, it must be outside of school, and student must be of legal age)

dyslexia

dysthymia

emotional disorders

excessive absenteeism

HIV/AIDS

injuries

medical conditions (asthma, allergies, diabetes, heart disease, cancer, hemophilia)

mutism

obesity

physical/sexual abuse

posttraumatic stress syndrome

sexually transmitted diseases

suicidal tendencies

temporary conditions due to illness or accident

temporary illnesses

tuberculosis

How Section 504 Is Different from IDEA

All individuals who are disabled or "handicapped" are protected under Section 504. However, individuals who have been determined to be "handicapped" under Section 504 may not be considered disabled under IDEA. IDEA, which can be viewed as a subcategory of Section 504, provides for special programming or placement, while Section 504 protects the rights of individuals with handicaps. Under IDEA, students are qualified for services under 13 IDEA disabling conditions; specially designed individual education programs are planned for each student by Individualized Education Program (IEP) teams. Under Section 504, students with "handicaps" are entitled to special accommodations to ensure that they can participate in and benefit from public education and programs, and a 504 accommodation plan is designed for each student according to individual need.

Both Section 504 and IDEA require districts to provide a free appropriate public education (FAPE) to eligible students, including individually designed instruction. While IDEA requires a written IEP document, Section 504 requires that a plan—not necessarily an IEP—be developed and implemented. This plan must be developed by a group of people who know the student, and districts are strongly recommended to document that such a group has convened and specified the agreed-upon services detailed in the plan.

It is important to realize that Section 504 is not an aspect of special education, but is, rather, a responsibility of the comprehensive general public education system. Under IDEA, students are eligible for services only if their disability adversely affects educational performance; under Section 504, students are eligible for accommodations even if their disability does not negatively affect their educational performance. To be eligible for accommodations under Section 504, students need only meet the definitions for "handicap": having or having had a physical or mental impairment that substantially limits a major life activity, or being regarded as "handicapped" by others (see definitions above).

Of particular importance is the difference in funding for IDEA and Section 504. Under IDEA, districts receive additional funding for eligible students, while Section 504 does not provide additional funds. Further, IDEA funds may not be used to serve students eligible only under Section 504.

While both IDEA and Section 504 provide for certain procedural safeguards, those for IDEA are more stringent than those for 504. For instance, both require written notice to the parent or guardian regarding identification, evaluation, and/or placement. However, under Section 504 the notice need not be written, while under IDEA, the notice must be in written form. In spite of the differences in these procedural aspects, we strongly recommend that anyone developing 504 plans engage in the good professional practice inherent in the IDEA procedures. In the chapter to follow, we describe several examples of the 504 process—some resulting in 504 plans and some not—and detail the procedures and processes we found to be the most comprehensive and successful.

Both IDEA and Section 504 require evaluations. The IDEA evaluation is conducted by a multidisciplinary team or group, while the 504 evaluation is carried out by a group of people knowledgeable about the student, the evaluation data (which are drawn from a variety of sources in the area of concern), and placement options. Districts are required to evaluate particular students if the district has any reason to believe that because they have a "handicap" (as defined under Section 504), they need accommodations or services in the regular classroom setting. The evaluation need not necessarily be as comprehensive as a full special education evaluation. However, the evaluation must be "sufficient to accurately and completely assess the nature and extent of the handicap and the recommended services" (Council for Administrators of Special Education, 1992, p. 2). If the student is determined to fit the criteria for eligibility under Section 504, the district must develop and implement a plan to provide the needed services. It is important to know that these steps must be taken regardless of whether the student qualifies for services under IDEA.

Placement procedures are the same under both laws; however, to change placement under IDEA requires an IEP review meeting, while Section 504 requires a meeting to make a significant change to a student's placement (e.g., from elementary school to middle school, or from one teacher to another outside the normal change that is made when moving from one grade to another, or when a change in the 504 plan necessitates a change in the student's placement), and to discontinue Section 504 coverage for a student.

Grievance procedures differ, as well. Section 504 requires districts with more than 15 employees to assign an employee to be responsible for district compliance with Section 504 and to develop a grievance procedure for parents, students, and employees.

IDEA does not provide for either a grievance procedure or a compliance officer. Both IDEA and 504 provide for due process; however, the IDEA procedures are specifically delineated, while the 504 procedures are less specific.

As we mentioned earlier, IDEA is enforced by the U.S. Office of Special Education Programs, and compliance is monitored by the State Department of Education and the Office of Special Education programs. All complaints under IDEA are resolved by the State Department of Education. Section 504 is enforced by the U.S. Office of Civil Rights; the State Department of Education has no involvement in monitoring or the resolution of complaints.

While special education teachers and administrators are participants in the 504 process, the primary responsibility for Section 504 rests with the local education agency administration. Many states have developed state-level regulations regarding Section 504 that may further delineate the processes involved in implementing Section 504 plans. To find out if your state has its own regulations regarding Section 504, contact the state education agency for information.

Table 1.1 provides an overview of the similarities and differences between IDEA and Section 504.

(*text continues on page 10*)

Table 1.1
Comparison of IDEA and Section 504

Component	IDEA	Section 504
General Purpose	Is a federal funding statute whose purpose is to provide financial aid to states in their efforts to ensure adequate and appropriate services for disabled children.	Is a broad civil rights law that protects the rights of individuals with handicaps in programs and activities that receive Federal financial assistance from the U.S. Department of Education.
Who Is Protected?	Identifies all school-aged children who fall within one or more specific categories of qualifying conditions.	Identifies all school-age children who meet the definition of qualified handicapped person, i.e., (1) has or (2) has had a physical or mental impairment that substantially limits a major life activity, or (3) is regarded as handicapped by others. Major life activities include walking, learning, hearing, speaking, breathing, learning, working, caring for oneself and performing manual tasks. The handicapping condition need only substantially limit one major life activity in order for the student to be eligible.

(continues)

Table 1.1 Continued.

Component	IDEA	Section 504
Responsibility to Provide a Free and Appropriate Public Education (FAPE)	Both laws require the provision of a free appropriate public education to eligible students covered under them, including individually designed instruction. The Individual Education Program (IEP) of IDEA will suffice for Section 504 written plan.	
	Requires a written IEP document with specific content and a required number of specific participants at the IEP meeting.	Does not require a written IEP document but does require a plan. It is recommended that the district document that a group of persons knowledgeable about the student convened and specified agreed-upon services.
	"Appropriate education" means a program designed to provide "educational benefit." Related services are provided if required for the student to benefit from specially designed instruction.	"Appropriate" means an education comparable to the education provided to non-handicapped students, requiring that reasonable accommodations be made. Related services, independent of any special education services as defined under IDEA, may be the reasonable accommodation.
Special Education vs. Regular Education	A student is only eligible to receive IDEA services if the multi-disciplinary team determines that the student is disabled under one or more of the specific qualifying conditions and requires specially designed instruction to benefit from education.	A student is eligible so long as s/he meets the definition of qualifed handicapped person; i.e., (1) has or (2) has had a physical or mental impairment that substantially limits a major life activity, or (3) is regarded as handicapped by others. It is not required that the handicap adversely affect educational performance, or that the student need special education in order to be protected.
Funding	Provides additional funding for eligible students.	Does not provide additional funds. IDEA funds may not be used to serve children found eligible only under Section 504.
Accessibility	Requires that modifications must be made if necessary to provide access to a free appropriate education.	Has regulations regarding building and program accessibility, requiring that reasonable accommodations be made.
Procedural Safeguards	Both require notice to the parent or guardian regarding identification, evaluation, and/or placement. IDEA procedures will suffice for Section 504 implementation.	

(continues)

Table 1.1 Continued.

Component	IDEA	Section 504
	Requires written notice.	Does not require written notice, but a district would be wise to do so.
	Delineates required components of written notice.	Written notice not required, but is indicated by good professional practice.
	Requires written notice prior to any change in placement.	Requires notice only before a "significant change" in placement.
Evaluations	A full comprehensive evaluation is required, assessing all areas related to the suspected disability. The child is evaluated by a multidisciplinary team or group.	Evaluation draws on information from a variety of sources in the area of concern; decisions made by a group knowledgeable about the student, evaluation data, and placement options.
	Requires informed consent before an initial evaluaton is conducted.	Does not require consent, only notice. However, good professional practice indicates informed consent.
	Requires re-evaluations to be conducted at least every 3 years.	Requires periodic re-evaluations. IDEA schedule for re-evaluation will suffice.
	A re-evaluation is not required before a significant change in placement. However, a review of current evaluation data, including progress monitoring, is strongly recommended.	Re-evaluation is required before a significant change in placement.
	Provides for independent educational evaluation at district expense if parent disagrees with evaluation obtained by school and hearing officer concurs.	No provision for independent evaluation at district expense. District should consider any such evaluations presented.
Placement Procedures	When interpreting evaluation data and making placement decisions, both laws require districts to:	

a. Draw upon information from a variety of sources;

b. Assure that all information is documented and considered;

c. Ensure that the eligibility decision is made by a group of persons, including those who are knowledgeable about the child, the meaning of the evaluation data, and placement options;

d. Ensure that the student is educated with her/his nonhandicapped peers to the maximum extent appropriate (least restrictive environment).

| | An IEP review meeting is required before any change in placement. | A meeting is not required for any change in placement. |

(continues)

Table 1.1 Continued.

Component	IDEA	Section 504
Grievance Procedure	Does not require a grievance procedure, nor a compliance officer.	Requires districts with more than 15 employees to (1) designate an employee to be responsible for assuring district compliance with Section 504 and (2) provide a grievance procedure for parents, students, and employees.
Due Process	Both statutes require districts to provide impartial hearings for parents or guardians who disagree with the identification, evaluation, or placement of a student.	
	Delineates specific requirements.	Requires that the parent have an opportunity to participate and be represented by counsel. Other details are left to the discretion of the local school district. Policy statements should clarify specific details.
Exhaustion	Requires the parent or guardian to pursue administrative hearing before seeking redress in the courts.	Administrative hearing not required prior to OCR involvement or court action; compensatory damages possible.
Enforcement	Enforced by the U.S. Office of Special Education Programs. Compliance is monitored by the State Department of Education and the Office of Special Education Programs.	Enforced by the U.S. Office of Civil Rights.
	The State Department of Education resolves complaints.	State Department of Education has no monitoring, complaint resolution, or funding involvement.

Note. From *Student Access: A Resource Guide for Educators* (pp. 4–7), by the Council of Administrators of Special Education, undated, Reston, VA: Council for Exceptional Children. Copyright 1992 by the Council for Exceptional Children. Reprinted with permission.

Why Section 504 Is Reemerging Now

Before the Vietnam War most laws mandating equal access and special services for persons with disabilities focused on *physical* disabilities. Prompted by the large numbers of wounded and disabled soldiers returning to this country following both World War I and World War II, the U.S. Congress passed significant laws regarding physical disabilities. After Vietnam, however, when many soldiers returned to this country suffering from significant physical *and* mental disabilities, we were forced to rethink our concept of disability. Many veterans and their advocates fought fierce battles to gain access to jobs and services to which they felt entitled. They forced us to think, perhaps for the first time, of disability in political terms (Smith and Luckesson, 1995).

In response, Congress passed the Rehabilitation Act of 1973, which included Section 504, a set of regulations attempting to eliminate discrimination against people with disabilities in workplaces and schools. While Section 504 mandated "comparable" education and access for students with "handicaps," it did not provide federal funds to states to implement the law. When Congress passed P.L. 94-142 (now called IDEA) two years later, in 1975, and provided for additional federal funding to support special services for eligible students, Section 504 was largely forgotten. Section 504 plans were used primarily to make temporary adjustments for students with health or medical needs (e.g., a temporarily shortened day for a student returning from surgery or a modified physical education curriculum for a student with physical limitations).

There are three primary reasons why Section 504 has been rediscovered. The first—and probably the most influential—is the inclusion movement. In the 1980s, the philosophical and political shift from the concept of "mainstreaming" to that of "inclusion" refocused attention on how educational practices in the regular classroom affected students with disabilities. Even though IDEA mandated education in the least restrictive environment (LRE), segregated special education services were still the norm in 1980. Ironically, the students receiving the most segregated services generated the most funds for school districts.

Additionally, the concept of mainstreaming was based on the belief that children with disabilities should be educated in segregated placements until they could "swim" in the mainstream of public education. General educators were neither trained nor expected to modify their teaching practices to accommodate these students. It is not surprising that few children, once placed, exited from special education programs into the mainstream. When they did, they frequently failed.

With the advent of the inclusion movement—spearheaded by the parents of and persons with physical disabilities—thinking shifted to the belief that all children should be educated in the regular classrooms they would have attended if no disabilities existed. Under the concept of inclusion, any services provided in a separate room or in a school other than the person's home school must be justified by the need and best interest of the individual child. Scruggs and Mastropieri (1994) have identified the following critical dimensions that have been found in schools where effective inclusion has occurred:

- Administrative support is apparent.
- Special education support exists.
- Open, accepting classroom atmosphere is evident.
- Appropriate curriculum is operative.
- Effective general teaching skills are displayed.
- Peer assistance is available.
- Disability-specific teaching skills are used when necessary.

While many grants and pilot projects have been funded to try inclusion in the schools, basic funding mechanisms and mainstreaming practices have remained. Nevertheless, the belief in inclusion as a basic democratic right remains a strong one in the disability community and continues to fuel educational reform.

A second force in the movement toward the use of Section 504 is the increase in and awareness of persons with mental or physical disabilities who do not qualify for special education services under the eligibility rules of IDEA. The largest group of these children are those who have been diagnosed with ADHD. Advocacy groups such as CHADD, having been unsuccessful in having ADHD added to the eligibility categories for services under IDEA, have increasingly turned to the Rehabilitation Act of 1973 and Section 504 for relief. In addition, the recognition that unmet mental health needs present a major barrier to school success for many of our children has prompted the move to link schools with community health providers. In the past few years, schools have been pressured to develop and implement 504 modification plans for a diverse population of students who, because of an identified or perceived disabling condition, are not benefitting from the instruction they currently receive.

A third reality that is encouraging the increased use of Section 504 is the widespread criticism special education has come under in recent years. Some of the criticism centers on the fact that the cumbersome and invasive process of referral, evaluation, labeling, and placement in special education of students with disabilities actually exacerbates the problems it is designed to relieve. The shortage of well-trained special education teachers has contributed to this concern. Outcome studies of students with mild-to-moderate learning disabilities have led many parents and educators to believe that their students would be better off left in the mainstream to "sink or swim" than to be separated, stigmatized, and then educated with sometimes questionable educational practices.

What Section 504 Offers

In view of the history of special education and the current climate in schools, aspects of the Rehabilitation Act and Section 504 that were once considered weaknesses of the law may be seen as assets. The Rehabilitation Act, including Section 504, is an unfunded mandate; that is, no additional funds are generated for the school if a 504 plan is developed for a student. What this means is that it is impossible for a student with a disability to be identified and placed in a program in order to fill a quota that generates funds for a school district—a common practice under the federally funded IDEA legislation.

Because of the lack of additional funding, many states and districts have been reluctant to make families and students fully aware of their right to receive modifications under Section 504. Once spurned as making general educators too accountable for the educational care of students with disabilities, Section 504 is now being embraced for that very reason. The general belief that special teachers with highly specialized training are required to teach children with disabilities (or "handicaps") crumbles in the face of the huge numbers of children who do not appear to be benefitting from specialized education.

As we will discuss in a later section, technically, students protected by Section 504 *can* receive special education services; however, those services cannot be paid for with

IDEA monies. What this means is that the responsibility for implemention of modifi-cations for students under 504 rests with general educators. Section 504 offers these teachers a clear documentation process for implementing modifications, as well as pro-viding for consistent and fair treatment of these students. Further, the use of Section 504 emphasizes the need for professional development and technical assistance for the general classroom teacher.

Section 504 is intended to level the playing field for students facing life chal-lenges. When it is introduced, implemented, and supported properly, a 504 plan can facilitate significant improvement in school success for all students by supporting good professional development and the institutionalization of inclusive teaching practices.

The Myth of the "Normal" Learner

One of the major corollaries of the inclusive school movement is the increasing under-standing that there is no such thing as a "normal" learner. As school communities moved from mainstreaming to inclusion, teachers began to view their students as indi-vidual learners rather than groups of "normal" learners, groups of those "below nor-mal," and groups of students "above normal." By seeing students as individual learners with individual instructional needs, teachers could let go of the notion that their instruction could be aimed at "the norm." Instead, many teachers undertook the pro-cess of individualizing instruction to meet the myriad learning needs represented by all of the students in their classrooms, not just those arriving with IEPs.

Many teachers were aided in their efforts to tailor instruction to student needs by the explosion of information about learning styles, by the emergence and validation of the theory of multiple intelligences, and by the establishment of good teaching prac-tices associated with magnet schools, schools within schools, and charter schools, to name just a few.

What we in education know now, as we approach a new millennium, is that instruction succeeds to the extent that it is rendered interesting to the student, rele-vant to the student, and connected with the experiences of the student. In a very important way, Section 504 plans formalize what we know as good teaching practice: a group of people who know the student and care primarily about the student's success (including the student, if possible) develop an instructional plan for the student, tak-ing into consideration the student's unique strengths and needs as a learner and as a person. This same group of people formulates a process detailing how the plan will be implemented and by whom, how it will be evaluated and modified, and when each phase will occur. While Section 504 plans give us a means by which we can empha-size our commitment to students who now have a disability, have had a disability, or are regarded as having a disability, these plans can be used as a means to emphasize our commitment to *all* students.

We are not advocating that every student have a Section 504 plan. What we *are* recommending, however, is that teachers use the 504 planning process as a model for how they approach instruction in general. The 504 planning process moves us away from emphasis on a narrow group of learners deemed "normal" and toward concentration on developing instruction tailored to meet each student's unique learning needs.

Focus on Strengths

While Section 504 provides a means for preventing discrimination against students with disabilities, this does not mean that 504 plans must focus on the disabling condition or on addressing the disability directly. Rather, 504 plans offer a means for focusing on students' strengths, for capitalizing on what students bring to the instructional process—not on what they lack. You will see in the stories and sample plans we have included in later sections that students' disabilities are not at the center of the planning process. Rather, the plans we include here are exemplars of focusing on students' strengths and capabilities in our efforts to devise ways for them to achieve their potentials.

As we said earlier, our approach in using Section 504 planning is that to focus on disorder or what students lack is to miss entirely the point of instruction designed to accommodate student needs. Emphasis on disorder leads to a "glass half empty" perspective, in which instruction is geared to fixing something that is considered to be wrong. Emphasis on strength, on the other hand, leads to a "glass half full" view, in which students are seen as competent learners and instruction is designed to help students move from where they are to where they want (and their families want them) to be: in position to be contributing and responsible citizens participating in and benefitting from life in their communities.

We invite you to consider these thoughts as you think about strengths.

What Are Strengths?

- Strengths are what people have learned about themselves, others, and their world as they have struggled, coped, and battled abuse, trauma, illness, confusion, oppression, and their own fallibility. People do learn from their trials, even those that they inflict upon themselves. People learn not only from their successes but from their disappointments and difficulties as well.

- Strengths are what people know about the world around them, from that which they have gathered intellectually or educationally to those things they have discerned and distilled through their life experiences. Perhaps they have developed skill at spotting incipient interpersonal conflict; maybe they have developed a capacity to soothe others who are suffering. It could be that they can use art and literature to teach others about themselves; perhaps life has given them the opportunity to know how to tend to the needs of young children.

- Strengths are personal qualities and virtues that people possess that are sometimes forged and developed in the fires of trauma and trouble. A sense of humor, creative capacities, loyalty, insight, independence, interpersonal skills, and other traits might very well be the source of energy and direction in our work with particular individuals and groups.

- Strengths are the talents that people have that can surprise us (as well as surprising the individual when talents have long lain dormant). Playing a musical instrument, storytelling, cooking, auto repair, carpentry, writing—who knows what it might be—may provide tools and resources for helping individuals, families, and communities come closer to realizing their aspirations.

- Strengths often reside in cultural and personal stories and lore, which are often profound sources of strength, guidance, stability, and transformation and which are often overlooked. Cultural aproaches to helping—for example, the sweat lodge or medicine wheel, *curanderismo*, the role of fosterage among poor families—can be a foundation for helping. Cultural stories, narratives, and myths, accounts of origins and migrations, development and survival, may provide sources of inspiration and meaning. Personal and familial stories of falls from grace and redemption, of failure and resurrection, of struggle and resilience, may also provide the diction, metaphors, the clues to make life better.

- Strengths often show in pride. People who have surmounted obstacles and rebounded from adversity have pride that may be buried under blame, shame, marginalization, and labeling. Nevertheless, their pride is there waiting to be tapped. As the saying goes, "Pride drives the engine of change; shame jams the gears."

- Strengths are the communities in which we live. Communities are often overlooked as a source of resources, especially the informal or natural environments. Most communities and neighborhoods are full of people and institutions who, if asked, would provide their talents in the service of helping and supporting others.

- Finally, it is important to remember that people often forget what strengths and talents they once enjoyed and possessed. It is also important to note that sometimes people do not define their capacities and knowledge as strengths. (Adapted from Salleeby, 1997; used with permission)

Responsibilities to Students

Section 504 provides students with disabilities that significantly affect a major life activity the services and aids necessary for them to participate in and benefit from public instruction. In providing these services and aids, districts assume a set of responsibilities toward students and, indirectly, toward their families as well.

Identification

In order to receive the services offered under Section 504, students must be identified as having, having had, or being perceived as having a mental or physical impairment that interferes with a major life activity. Therefore, the district's responsibility is to design a set of procedures for identifying students who are eligible to receive assistance under Section 504.

Some discussion is necessary regarding what is perceived as a disability. For example, in one instance we know about, several students had been receiving special education services for two years because they had been diagnosed as having a language disorder, primarily as a result of learning English as a second language (their native language is Navajo). At present, they are being removed from special education because it has been determined that they do *not* have a language disorder, but rather that they are in need of English instruction. The question facing this district is whether these students are protected under Section 504 because, clearly, they have been treated as having a disability—they received special education services based on their identification as having a disability. Because of this situation, the district has taken the position that *any* student exiting special education services is protected under Section 504.

Along a slightly different line, we have become aware of several districts in which classroom teachers are voluntarily identifying and serving students with 504 plans. In each of these districts, a comprehensive plan has been developed to assist teachers in their efforts to identify students who qualify. In one district, for example, teachers receive information and materials about Section 504 as part of the beginning-of-school-year inservice devoted to improving teaching through tailoring instruction to student needs and strengths. The teachers are guided through a set of sample cases, designed to show how Section 504 can be used to support students' learning needs. In addition, the teachers receive the documentation materials necessary to demonstrate how they are using and complying with Section 504. Later in this book we will include examples of some of these materials.

In other districts, however, students are not identified unless someone—the student, a family member or guardian, or an advocate for the student—requests that a 504 plan be considered. In these districts, 504 plans are developed in response to a perceived problem, rather than as part of ongoing instructional delivery.

In either case, in the identification stage districts will want to appoint the school site administrator or designee to convene a group of persons knowledgeable about the student and the area of concern to determine whether a Section 504 referral is appropriate. If the referral is inappropriate (e.g., a student is currently being served under IDEA), the administrator will take the necessary steps to notify the person making the referral and document the decision. We will return to the documentation process when we discuss the 504 process in the next chapter and again in Chapter 5, where we will address developing Section 504 policies and procedures. If the referral is an appropriate one, i.e., the student's needs are not currently being met under another program, the administrator will want to establish a Section 504 committee of people who know the student and the area of concern and set a date, time, and place—preferably the student's school of attendance—for an evaluation meeting.

In some districts, parents/family members are considered an essential part of the committee, while in other districts, parents are invited to participate but are not considered part of the decision making.

Evaluation and Periodic Reevaluations

Once a student has been identified and referred for a Section 504 plan, an evaluation must take place in order to determine what, if any, accommodations would benefit the student. As we have said earlier, the committee appointed to perform the evaluation must include persons knowledgeable about the student, the meaning of the evaluation data, the placement options, and the legal requirement to place a student with a disability in the least restrictive environment. Ideally, the student's teacher(s) would be on the evaluation committee.

The committee is responsible for gathering and reviewing data about the student and her or his learning needs, to notify the parents or family of the results of the evaluation, and to work with the teacher(s) of the student to ensure understanding of the recommended accommodation(s). The committee is also responsible for follow-up with the teacher(s) to determine that the recommended accommodations are implemented. In addition, the committee's responsibilities include scheduling reevaluations as needed in each individual student's case.

As we touched on earlier, CASE recommends that the evaluation be "sufficient to accurately and completely assess the nature and extent of the handicap, and the recommended services" (Council for Administrators of Special Education, 1992, p. 2). While a full special education evaluation may be indicated, a more limited evaluation may be adequate in some cases. For instance, CASE describes the case of a student with juvenile arthritis for whom the evaluation might consist of the parents and school nurse meeting to review the student's medical records (Council for Administrators of Special Education, 1992). In another instance, for a student with Attention-Deficit Disorder (ADD), CASE describes the evaluation as consisting of a review of current psychoeducational assessments in combination with appropriate medical information related to the ADD (Council for Administrators of Special Education, 1992).

If further evaluation is deemed necessary, it must be conducted in the student's native language, and the evaluation must be individualized to each particular student.

Placement

Under Section 504, most accommodations take place in the student's school of attendance, and within the student's classroom. However, if the committee overseeing the student's 504 plan determines that the student will benefit most from, and be served in the least restrictive environment in, a setting different from his or her home school or classroom, alternative placement can be an option. What Section 504 plans require is that the placement provide facilities and services comparable to those provided to nondisabled (or "nonhandicapped") students. In addition, 504 plans must ensure that the placement provide the student a free appropriate public education designed to meet her or his individual educational needs as adequately as the needs of students without disabilities are met.

Discipline

Disciplining students who are receiving accommodations under a Section 504 plan has become a critical issue in many districts and states. There are two crucial aspects to consider in the disciplining of students with disabilities. The first is whether a student's misconduct is a manifestation of the student's disability; the second is whether a disciplinary action constitutes a significant change in placement.

If any student under a 504 plan engages in misconduct that would result in removal or exclusion from the student's normal (i.e., 504 plan) placement, the evaluation committee must reevaluate the student to determine whether the misconduct is related to a disability. The Office of Civil Rights has indicated that this reevaluation must be conducted by a group of persons knowledgeable about the student and that the evaluation may not be done unilaterally by one individual.

If the committee finds that the child's conduct is caused by a disability, the committee must further evaluate in order to determine whether the student's current educational placement is appropriate. Nonpunitive placement changes may be made if they would be more appropriate and better serve the student's needs. However, punitive placement changes may not be made unless the committee determines that the misconduct is not related to the student's disability. If this is the case, the student may be excluded from school in the same manner as a student without disabilities.

It should be noted, however, that in some states emergency placement or expulsion can occur if it is believed that the student's behavior is so unruly or disruptive that it interferes with the teacher's effectiveness or with other students' learning, or if persons or property are in danger of imminent harm.

Section 504 makes an exception in its disciplinary requirements for students who are engaged in the illegal use of drugs or alcohol. These students are subject to the same disciplinary actions as students without disabilities, and parents or families may not resort to due process procedures to contest the disciplinary action.

Accommodations and Modifications

Accommodations/modifications constitute one of the most important pieces of the 504 plan. Modifications must be designed to increase the opportunities for success for the student. Effective modifications include an emphasis on the following:

1. *Strengths*. As we discussed in an earlier section, we urge an emphasis on the student's strengths. In considering modifications, ask these questions:

- What is going well for the student, and how can you build on that success?

- What are this student's interest areas, and how can they be used to increase success in learning?

- What does this student seek out to attend to?

- How might problem behaviors inform us about this student's needs?

- How can we build on assets in this situation (e.g., who in the family is available for support) to help this student meet her or his needs?

2. *Least intrusive intervention.* Modifications should be designed to be as close to the general classroom procedures and methods as possible. For example, a modification might consist of having the student do every other math problem in a math assignment rather than giving the student a different assignment entirely. In addition, smaller modifications should be tried before larger, more complicated ones are attempted (Doudy, Patton, Smith, & Polloway, 1997).

3. *Customizing the description of the modification(s).* Section 504 plan modifications should be described in terms that encourage teachers to implement in a way that makes sense for their program. For example, one modification might be described as "allow a reasonable amount of time for assignments to be turned in after the official due date" instead of stated in specific terms, e.g., "work can be turned in two days late." Different assignments, curricula, and teaching methods need different adjustments, which are made possible by descriptions that, while focusing on the student's needs, also fit teachers and classrooms.

4. *Considering academic modifications first.* When a student feels that the demands being placed on him or her are overwhelming, frustration and fear often manifest themselves as misbehavior. By adjusting academic expectations, behavior issues often diminish or disappear completely.

5. *Matching the modification to the need and choosing only those modifications that are needed.* For example, if a student is doing well in one subject, consider carefully that perhaps no modification is needed in that subject at that particular time. In other words, don't fix what isn't broken.

6. *Prioritizing and implementing only a few modifications at a time.* In our experience, specifying multiple modifications at one time often overwhelms teachers, parents or families, and the student. Choose three or four modifications to address the most pressing needs, and use follow-up committee/team meetings to make needed adjustments. In addition to making the modification plans reasonable and manageable, limiting choices to a few changes at a time helps the committee/team better assess the effectiveness of the plan. If too many changes are implemented at once, it is very difficult to sort out which changes are having which effects.

7. *Reviewing and adjusting.* The process of designing and implementing modifications for success should be viewed as an ongoing process, which, like any process, needs to be evaluated periodically. The committee/team needs to agree on an appropriate interval for scheduling reviews: every month, 6 weeks, 9 weeks, and so forth. By reviewing periodically, the modification plan can be adjusted and fine-tuned before long intervals of time have passed, during which the plan may or may not be succeeding.

Program Accessibility

Section 504 is clear in its insistence that students who are being served under the law must have access to programs, activities, and physical locations equal to the access provided to students without disabilities. In other words, Section 504 students may not be discriminated against by providing services, for instance, in inferior facilities, such as trailers, basements, or unnecessarily restrictive classrooms. In addition, if the committee/team determines that the best services in the least restrictive environment for a particular student exist at a location other than the student's home school, the district must offer those services. In addition, if such a program is not operated by the district, the district must provide transportation to and from the alternative placement setting at no greater cost than would be incurred if the student were placed in a district-operated program.

Under Section 504, districts must guarantee meaningful access for students with disabilities to all school-initiated activities, not just the academic ones. In other words, students must be given an equal opportunity to participate in all nonacademic and extracurricular activities offered by the district. In addition, parents with disabilities must be provided access to all activities sponsored by the district.

Due Process

With one exception, Section 504 guarantees students' families the right to a specified process by which they can appeal the decisions regarding identification, evaluation, placement, and change of placement of their children. (As noted earlier, the exception is for students who are currently using alcohol or drugs.) While not as stringent as the process required under IDEA, the process under Section 504 does protect students and their families from indiscriminate placement and/or expulsion or exclusion.

Section 504 requires a grievance procedure in districts with over 15 employees. The procedure includes the designation of an employee as the officer ensuring district compliance with Section 504, as well as the provision of a grievance procedure for parents, students, and employees. In addition, districts are required to establish a due process by which families can disagree with or appeal the decisions of the Section 504 committee/team.

In general, due process includes a set of procedures for notification of families regarding any actions taken under Section 504: identifying a student who may be eligible for a 504 plan, evaluating the student, designing modification/determining placement, periodic reevaluations, and appealing decisions. In addition, due process includes procedures for families to appeal any of the Section 504 committee/team's decisions in regard to the identification, evaluation, or educational placement of their child. Parents/families have a right to request an impartial hearing, which typically involves a hearing officer appointed by the district to review district decisions related to the student; the officer may not be an employee of the district or under contract in any way to the district.

If either the district or the parents/family of the student disagree with the findings of the hearing officer, they have a right under Section 504 to seek a review of the officer's decision by a court of appropriate jurisdiction.

Figure 1.1 shows the IDEA/Section 504 Flow Chart developed by CASE (Council for Administrators of Special Education, 1992).

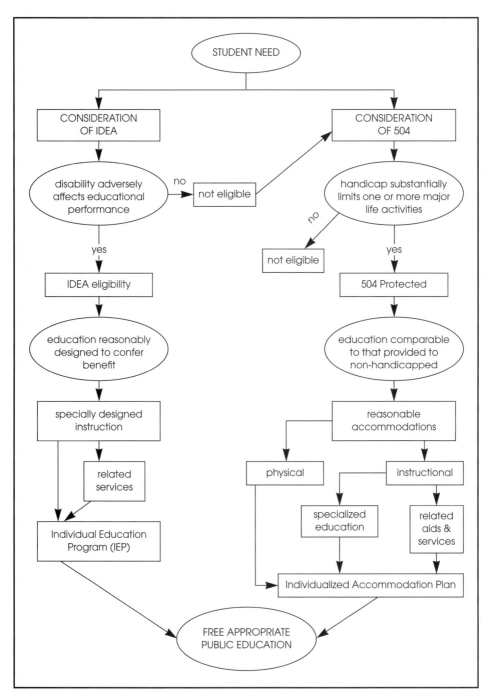

Figure 1.1. IDEA/Section 504 flow chart. *Note.* From *Student Access: A Resource Guide for Educators: Section 504 of the Rehabilitation Act of 1973* (p. 3a), by the Council of Administrators of Special Education, 1992. Reston, VA: Author. Copyright 1992 by the Council for Exceptional Children. Reprinted with permission.

Summary

In this chapter we have introduced Section 504 and presented the definitions and concepts associated with its use. We have provided a bit of historical background to show why Section 504 is reemerging in education after almost 25 years of residing in the shadow of IDEA and, before that, P.L. 94-142. To illustrate the regulations surrounding Section 504, we offered a comparison with the rules regulating IDEA. We concluded the chapter with a summary of responsibilities to students and their families that Section 504 confers on school districts.

The Section 504 Process

Andy is a 12-year-old boy in sixth grade at a middle school in a large, urban school district. He lives with his parents and his 5-year-old brother. Andy's parents are both professionals: his mother is a medical doctor, and his father is a retired school principal who currently is a successful business consultant and musician, having played professionally with a band for 20 years.

A tall, thin boy, Andy has a wild shock of blond hair. Andy's father shared that Andy was a somewhat unusual child, but that his family had always encouraged him to follow his own interests. In addition, the family was fairly loose with routines and rules when Andy was young.

Andy experienced difficulties from the time he started school, which he didn't like. His parents placed him at a private Montessori school for second, third, and fourth grades. In third grade, Andy was diagnosed with ADHD and placed on Ritalin, which greatly improved his ability to focus outside his own interests. It also helped him comply better with school demands.

Since he was a small child, Andy's interests have centered on the natural world. He still spends his free time along the acequia system that runs along the river behind his home. He knows detailed information about the insects, water life, and birds in this habitat, and he reads natural history on his own. Though Andy has had a few successful friendships outside his family, he usually plays with boys who share his interest in the natural world.

For fifth grade Andy's parents moved him back to the public school in his neighborhood and began taking him to a private therapist. He had a rough year during fifth grade, and the family was concerned about facing middle school. Before the next school year began, Andy began showing signs of depression, he became very irritable, and he talked about suicide. The therapist referred the family to a psychiatrist, who prescribed an antidepressant.

Andy started middle school where classes are organized into "families" of four teachers who work with the same group of students throughout the day. Although at first everything seemed manageable for Andy, after a few weeks he began to have problems adjusting. His grades on the first report card were D's and F's, except for band, which he loved, and where he was learning to play clarinet. Andy's teachers thought he must be gifted in some way and that he just could not function in school. In addition, his teachers did not believe he should be referred for special education because the school is a full-inclusion school, and they believed Andy was too bright for special education.

Meanwhile, Andy's problems escalated. Many days he "forgot" to go to the nurse to take his noon medications. Consequently, on these days the afternoons were what his teachers called "wild." Andy would talk out in class or refuse to work. One day he brought a pet snake to school in his backpack, apparently in an attempt to impress his classmates, who had begun to tease and harass him. On several occasions Andy ran away from school, and when other children attacked him verbally on the bus, he began to fight back.

In addition, Andy was unable to keep up with the written work, even though his father was at home to help him almost every afternoon after school. Andy frequently hid his work or "lost" it. He was confused, disorganized, and unhappy. Eventually, he began to act out in class, primarily in inattentive rather than disruptive ways. Neither his parents nor his teachers knew what to do. His parents were considering sending him to a boarding school in another state that specialized in experiential education for children who learn differently—mainly boys with learning and emotional problems who had failed in public schools.

At that time the family was referred to a pilot program in the public school that provided a behavioral/educational consultant to help in situations in which students in general education settings were having adjustment problems related to a specific problem such as depression or ADHD. The consultant first met privately with Andy's father to discuss his history, to learn about his strengths and learning styles, and to hear about the family's and school's concerns. The consultant then observed Andy in several classes and met with all of his teachers during their common preparation period.

Following these meetings and observations, the consultant made three recommendations for Andy, one of which was to develop and implement a Section 504 plan, which none of Andy's teachers or parents were aware of, to modify current classroom demands. The other two recommendations were to carefully review and assess the effectiveness of Andy's stimulant and antidepressant medications and to obtain a complete neuropsychological evaluation to assess Andy's learning systems.

While the medication and neuropsychological evaluations were being conducted, the consultant continued to talk with Andy's parents, as well as to meet with his teachers to explore which modifications might be helpful for Andy and be considered reasonable by his teachers. The consultant provided the team with suggestions and materials related to ADHD and depression in children and adolescents, and she discussed Andy's strengths and needs with the team. In addition, the team explored modifications and accommodations they believed would be helpful to Andy.

A 504 planning meeting was scheduled, during which Andy's parents, all of his core curriculum teachers (the "team"), the building principal, the neuropsychologist who had evaluated Andy, and the consultant reviewed the evaluation results and developed a plan for Andy, which is shown in Figure 2.1. Though Andy did not want to attend the meeting, he was briefed afterward by his father.

Section 504 Plan

Lynda Miller, Ph.D.   Chris Newbill, Ph.D.

I. REFERRAL DOCUMENTATION

1. General Information

Student Name __Andy__ Birth Date __2/7/84__ Today's Date __11/6/96__

Address _____ City _____ State _____ Zip _____

Parent(s) Name(s) _____ Home Phone _____ Work Phone _____

504 Coordinator _____ Phone _____

2. Referral

1. Is there a disability/handicap present that substantially limits one or more major life activities?

   Yes ☒ No ☐   If yes, which major life activity is limited? (check one or more, as appropriate)

   ☐ caring for self   ☐ walking   ☐ seeing

   ☐ hearing   ☐ speaking   ☐ breathing

   ☒ learning   ☐ working   ☐ other (describe) _____

2. Describe the nature of the concern. __Andy has had ADHD since third grade and currently takes Ritalin. He has trouble concentrating and focusing on certain academic tasks, especially math and written language.__

3. Describe how the disability/handicap affects a major life activity. __Andy's teachers have observed him "lose" his assignments and homework, and he sometimes "forgets" to go to the nurse for his noon medication. Andy has difficulties with the workload required in math and written language.__

4. Evaluation required? Yes ☒ No ☐ Date __11/6/96__ Signed __Andy's core teachers__
   (person(s) making referral)

If yes, schedule a Section 504 evaluation meeting and provide the following items to the parent(s)/guardian(s).

	Date sent	Sent by
• Notice of Section 504 meeting	11/6/96	(team leader)
• Parent/student rights under Section 504	11/6/96	(team leader)
• Acknowledgment of receipt of above forms (and parent response to scheduled meeting)	11/15/96	

Date of Evaluation Meeting: __11/26/96__ Time of Meeting: __9:30 a.m.__

Location of Meeting: __T. Middle School__

Reason for Meeting: ☒ Initial Evaluation

☐ Periodic Reevaluation

☐ Reevaluation before significant change in placement

(continues)

Figure 2.1. Andy's Section 504 plan.

LIBRARY
UNIVERSITY OF ST. FRANCIS
JOLIET, ILLINOIS

II. EVALUATION AND ELIGIBILITY DOCUMENTATION

1. Review of Available Information (include test scores when appropriate)

1. Summarize present levels of performance in areas evaluated. _Andy's current performance is below grade-level in written language and math. Grades for the year so far are D's & F's._

2. Teacher reports/comments: _Andy struggles with any assignment related to written language and to math. He doesn't seem to understand math concepts. Though his verbal language seems adequate for his work, he can't seem to translate it into writing._

3. Areas of concern: _Primarily written language and math. Also some concerns about behavior and taking his medication for ADHD._

4. Health and development: _Andy was diagnosed with ADHD in third grade and currently takes Ritalin. Other health and developmental milestones seem age appropriate._

5. Further information needed? Yes ☐ No ☒

   a) If yes, what information is needed?

   b) Person responsible for obtaining information: _NA_

   c) Date, time, and place to reconvene committee: _NA_

6. Evaluation was conducted by: (list names)

   (Andy's teachers; his parents; the district 504 consultant/ coordinator)

2. Eligibility

1. Does the student have a limiting mental or physical condition? Yes ☒ No ☐

   If yes, which major life activity is limited? (see p. 1 for list of conditions) _learning_

2. Rank the severity of the impairment.

Mild			Severe	
1	2	3	④	5

3. Rank the duration of the impairment.

Short				Long
1	2	3	4	⑤

Figure 2.1. Continued.

3. Placement

    ☒ regular classes   ☐ regular classes AND accommodative services

    ☐ special education   ☐ special education AND accommodative services

4. Date, Time, and Location of
   Accommodation Plan Meeting: _11/27/96_   _9:30 a.m._   _T. Middle School_
                                              Date   Time   Location

III. SPECIFIC ACCOMMODATIONS NEEDED

1. Describe the specific accommodations planned for this student, including the person responsible for each.

Accommodations Needed	Responsible Party
(1) Andy will keep an assignment book checked by his teachers daily.	(1) All teachers & parents.
(2) Modify the state writing assessment to allow Andy to dictate his story; his assessment will be hand-scored by his English teacher.	(2) English teacher.
(3) Modify written assignments as needed.	(3) All teachers.
(4) Allow Andy to work on a computer as much as possible.	(4) All teachers.

2. Criteria to be used to evaluate the accommodation plan: _Grades, agenda book, teacher anecdotal reports; team meetings every 6 weeks._

3. Person(s) responsible for evaluating the accommodation plan: _All teachers; Andy's parents._

Figure 2.1. Continued.

SPECIFIC ACCOMMODATIONS (Cont'd)

4. Participants—the persons whose signatures appear below developed this accommodation plan:

Name	Title	Date
Ms. Flint	English	11/17/96
Mr. García	Science	11/17/96
Ms. Simon	Social Studies	11/17/96
Ms. Genessee	Math	11/17/96
Mr. & Mrs. Jones	Parents	11/17/96
Mr. Sánchez	School Section 504 Officer	11/17/96

5. Date for accommodation plan review/reassessment: 1/7/97

6. Person(s) responsible for accommodation plan review/reassessment: Core teachers; Andy's parents

7. Parent statements:

   ☒ I received a written notice of my rights under Section 504.

   ☒ I received notice of the Section 504 evaluation meeting.

   ☒ I received notice of the Section 504 accommodation plan meeting.

   ☒ I agree with the Section 504 plan as it is written.

   ☒ I understand that, if I disagree with the content of this plan, I have the right to ask for a Section 504 review meeting or impartial hearing by filing a written request with the district Section 504 coordinator.

   (signed & dated by Andy's parents)
   _____   _____
   Parent/guardian signature   Date

   _____   _____
   Parent/guardian signature   Date

ADDITIONAL NOTES

_____

_____

_____

_____

_____

_____

_____

_____

Figure 2.1. Continued.

As you can see from reviewing the plan in Figure 2.1, the Section 504 committee—those present at the meeting—identified a few modifications to try at first, all of which centered on helping Andy develop control over his own learning, even if extensive cues and support were needed at first. Because of the preliminary meetings and discussions prior to the actual 504 planning meeting, Andy's teachers better understood Andy's behavior and felt comfortable with the procedure. In addition, the neuropsychological evaluation had identified that Andy possessed superior verbal intelligence, while his nonverbal and social learning were significantly impaired. As a result, everyone agreed that the modifications should focus on improving home/school communication about assignments and expectations, as well as reducing the written production demands, which were clearly Andy's greatest academic stumbling block.

As you can see in Figure 2.1, the Section 504 plan for Andy focused on several modifications. First, the committee agreed that Andy needed to learn to use his assignment notebook to stay organized. It was agreed that his teachers would check his book daily to make sure that he had recorded all assignments accurately. Though everyone agreed that the goal for Andy was that he manage the book on his own, they also agreed that his teachers would begin the modification process by each initialing the book every period of the day. Then Andy's dad or mom would sit down with him after school and coach him until his assignments were complete and in organized folders for the next day.

The second set of modifications, necessary for the first to work, centered on reducing written language demands. These included modifying the state writing assessment, an extensive in-class writing and editing process that takes several weeks, to allow dictation at home and hand scoring. The test was modified to assess Andy's composition skills without making him write everything. In addition, written assignments were reduced by allowing oral dictation with Andy's dad's help at home, and by cutting the length of assignments wherever possible. Because the intent of Andy's 504 plan was not to micromanage his teachers' instruction, details and individual decisions about specific modifications on specific assignments were left for the teachers' professional judgments.

The committee also made some minor changes in Andy's schedule to allow time for him to practice keyboarding skills. Teachers agreed to use objective test formats—true/false, multiple choice, etc.—or to use oral essay questions wherever possible.

Andy's 504 plan was initiated and developed just before winter break, in mid-December over a one-month period. Andy's grades just prior to the development of his 504 plan were D's and F's. Following the development of the 504 plan, Andy's parents and teachers helped him understand that his current grades did not reflect their new understanding of and partnership with him. In fact, the consultant suggested a ritual burning of his report card to symbolize putting it in the past! The four core curriculum teachers scheduled regular team meetings approximately every 4–5 weeks to review Andy's 504 plan and to share stories and strategies.

When school resumed following winter break, Andy began to express to his family that he liked his teachers, that they were fair, and that he felt school was getting better. Of particular interest is that Andy attributed his improvement to his own efforts. At the end of the next grading period, his grades were B's and C's, and during this time his social life began to improve. His friendship with another sixth-grade boy became stronger, and they began to associate outside of school.

As the school year progressed, his core teachers began planning how to transfer strategies, insights, and the success and trust established during the sixth grade to Andy's seventh-grade teachers, who also work as a "family." When this was written, everyone agreed that teaching Andy, parenting Andy, and *being* Andy were still challenges. Nevertheless, no one felt like giving up—especially Andy.

How did the 504 process help? It provided a framework to focus on supporting Andy so he could experience success in learning and in negotiating middle school. In addition, the process helped Andy's teachers coordinate their efforts, communicate better with Andy's parents, and receive support when they felt discouraged. In Andy's situation, the process worked to keep him in the regular classroom where he could begin to participate more meaningfully and to benefit from his experiences there.

Before Section 504 Plans Are Developed

As you can see from Andy's story, developing a Section 504 plan is a multistep process that depends on each individual's needs and situation. In fact, several factors should be considered in preparation for developing the plan itself.

When To Consider a 504 Plan

Because Section 504 is intended to guarantee that students participate in and benefit from public school education, any time a student seems at risk for, or in the process of, losing participation in or the benefits of any of the activities associated with the public school experience, educators should consider the existence of a disability and possible Section 504 protection. The following situations should be considered possible risk factors:

- when a student shows a pattern of not benefitting from instruction
- when suspension or expulsion is being considered
- when retention is being considered
- when a student returns to school following a serious injury or illness
- when a student is referred for an evaluation under IDEA, but a decision is made not to conduct the evaluation
- when a student is referred for an evaluation but does not qualify for services under IDEA
- when a student exhibits a chronic health condition

- when a student is identified as "at risk" or shows the potential for dropping out of school
- when a disability of any kind is suspected
- when substance abuse is an issue
- when a new building or remodeling is being considered (Council for Administrators of Special Education, 1992)

In addition, we would add another set of situations:

- when a teacher or teachers feel a student is a problem
- when a teacher or teachers want to refer a student out of their classroom because they feel unable to deal with her or him
- when a student is absent regularly
- when a student regularly receives poor grades
- when a student's academic performance suddenly changes
- when a student's behavior changes noticeably
- when a student regularly appears tired or has low energy
- when parents/guardians express concern about their child
- when a student expresses concern or distress
- when a student appears depressed

In Andy's situation, his teachers thought of him as a problem, though none thought of referring him to special education because their school is a full-inclusion school. In addition, Andy's parents were concerned enough to be considering sending him to an out-of-state school. In addition, Andy had been diagnosed with two disabling conditions: ADHD and depression. Thus, he fit several of the factors listed above.

What Section 504 Provides

As we have emphasized, Section 504 is designed to prevent discrimination against students with mental or physical disability. To comply fully with Section 504, many districts have developed a process for ensuring compliance, while others are at the beginning stages of developing compliance procedures. We offer the following timetable to show what needs to occur at each step of the compliance process.

In the Preparatory Phase

1. Identify a Section 504 compliance officer for the district.
2. Identify and train a designated 504 facilitator for each school. Typically, this person is a teacher or administrator already on staff; sometimes this person is a community volunteer.

3. Identify and designate specific resources and support for teachers who will be implementing Section 504 plans in their classrooms. Examples of resources and support for teachers might include a district-wide consultant on Section 504, the establishment of common planning or preparation times for teachers to meet to discuss issues related to Section 504 plans, the development of a handbook containing district policies and procedures regarding Section 504, examples of 504 plans from other districts, examples of modifications and accommodations related to specific types of disabilities, information regarding disabling conditions, and scheduled meetings for teachers with the district Section 504 facilitator to provide information and answer questions.

Once Section 504 Procedures Are in Place

1. Give appropriate and timely notification to parents/families about the intent to develop a Section 504 plan.

2. Schedule continued meetings for teachers with the district Section 504 facilitator to discuss which strategies/modifications best support student success, with focus on the least intrusive modifications needed.

3. Make the district Section 504 facilitator available to meet with parents/families and the student—prior to the 504 meeting—to help identify the student's strengths and needs as well as everyone's concerns.

4. Schedule enough time for the 504 meeting so that a relaxed and positive discussion can take place and so that everyone can agree on modifications that are reasonable and achievable.

5. Focus the meeting on the goal of student success and self-management.

6. Set a review schedule to ensure that the plan is working.

After the 504 Plan Is Initiated

1. Continue to provide teachers with access to support and/or feedback about the modifications that are being implemented.

2. Continue scheduled communication between parents and staff about questions, successes, and ongoing effectiveness of the plan.

3. Review or modify the plan yearly to accommodate maturation and learning as well as different teaching styles and schedules.

Before developing a Section 504 plan, it is important to review what the plan provides. The first step is identification of a student with a handicap, followed by an evaluation performed by a group knowledgeable about the student and the student's situation. Once the evaluation is complete, this same group develops a plan for modifying instruction, curricular content, communication, expectations, rules and consequences, demands on the student, the environment, materials, and/or physical setting—all undertaken to accommodate the unique needs of the student. Periodic reevaluation is scheduled to ensure ongoing accommodation that allows the student to participate in and benefit from public school education.

The following list includes all of the necessary parts of a 504 plan.

Essential Components of a Section 504 Plan

1. referral information and source
2. referral review and parent notification
3. evaluation: present levels of performance (strengths and needs)
   a. parent information and concerns
   b. teacher reports/comments
   c. areas of concern
   d. health and developmental history
4. eligibility determination
5. reasonable accommodations
6. criteria for measuring accomplishment of plan
7. review/reassessment date
8. signatures of participants

Although Section 504 does not require an assessment of a student's strengths, it does mandate an evaluation of the student's needs. You will recall that in Chapter 1 we discussed the importance of focusing on student strengths as a means for identifying how best to design accommodations and modifications supportive of the student's needs. Our practice is to include, as part of the student's 504 plan, a Strengths/Needs Profile, including a description of the student's strengths and needs in the following areas:

- academic/intellectual
- social/emotional
- motoric
- creative

There are many ways to describe students' strengths; we have chosen this organizational scheme because it is relatively brief and because it includes our areas of concern. As an example, Figure 2.2 shows a Strengths/Needs Profile for Andy.

The Section 504 Evaluation

To reiterate what we have said several times in earlier sections: first, what is required for a Section 504 evaluation is determined by the nature of the disability thought to be present as well as by the type of services the student might need. Second, Section 504 requires that the evaluation be overseen by a person or persons who know the student and the student's situation. And, third, the evaluation may consist of a review of existing information and data, or it may consist of additional testing and assessment. The defining criterion for the evaluation is that it be based on current levels of performance, teacher reports, and documentation of concern.

Strengths/Needs Profile

Name __Andy_____ DOB __2/7/84____ ID# _____

School __T. Middle School_____ Grade __6_____

This form completed by (name and title) _____

Please describe the strengths and needs of this child in the following areas. Information given here should be drawn from a variety of sources, such as school records, student self-reports, portfolio samples, teacher and parent anecdotal information, grades, any special recognition, and intra-/extracurricular activities.

Intellectual/Academic:

Strengths: Andy is a good reader, especially when the material is about a subject of interest to him. He is fascinated by the natural world of insects and fish that inhabit the irrigation ditches behind his home. He knows a great deal of factual information about a variety of animals. Andy is able to think divergently about topics of interest to him and gets very excited about trying experiments on his own. He is very verbal and linguistic; he loves to talk about things he's curious about.

Needs: Andy struggles when he must turn his thoughts and language into written text. He has difficulty with the multiple memory and motor demands of writing. In addition, Andy finds it hard to persevere when the task at hand requires great concentration, is assigned by someone else, or is not a topic of his own choosing. He is learning to type and uses a word processor, which reduces the mental load he experiences when writing; however, he still needs time and support to get written work finished. Andy has great difficulty learning numbers and number theory. Numbers seem to hold little meaning for him, which results in his having to work very hard to grasp math concepts.

Social/Emotional:

Strengths: Andy is a very sensitive person and has a loving, supportive family who have been eager to work with his teachers. They work with Andy every day after school to help him process the day's content and to complete his assignments. Andy's parents have provided him with the care, both physical and psychological, that he has needed to cope with social and developmental challenges. Andy has a strong inner locus of control, attributing success to his own efforts.

Needs: Andy has great difficulty reading social situations and understanding unspoken social cues. He sometimes appears immature to others in his

(*continues*)

Figure 2.2. Andy's Strengths/Needs Profile.

efforts to fit in socially. If he becomes overwhelmed and anxious in a complex social situation, he may withdraw or act silly in an effort to regain a state of comfort. His teachers have learned to notice signs of stress in Andy and to give him a break to regroup. They might do this by giving him an errand to run or by shortening an assignment so he has less to struggle with at a given time.

Motoric:

Strengths: Andy spends a great deal of his time outdoors. While he is not interested in team sports, he does a lot of physical exploration of the environment in which he lives. He attends a training class with his dog and has benefitted from the spatial awareness incorporated into the animal training.

Creative:

Strengths: Andy plays the clarinet. He has made great progress on this instrument and plays in the school band. He uses music and playing his instrument to unwind at the end of the school day. Andy has shown interest in many creative activities, especially when they involve exploring or illustrating the natural world.

Figure 2.2. Continued.

The "Knowledgeable" Group

Section 504 is clear in its requirement that an evaluation be overseen by people who know the student. In the case study of Andy with which we began this chapter, we pointed out that the evaluation was performed by Andy's parents, his core curriculum teacher, the educational/behavioral consultant who had spent time with Andy and his family, and the professional who administered the neuropsychological testing. Of this group, certainly Andy's family and teachers knew him well, while the consultant was familiar with his situation and needs through her conversations with Andy's mother and father, her discussions with Andy and her observations in his classes, and her conversations with his teachers. Because of her knowledge of Andy's needs, the consultant recommended the neuropsychological testing to gather pertinent information regarding Andy's learning and processing styles.

What To Include in the Evaluation

Because each student's situation will be different, it is impossible to state beforehand exactly what must be included in the Section 504 evaluation. Nevertheless, it is possible to draw some general guidelines for the evaluation process. The evaluation must concentrate on current levels of performance, teacher reports, and documentation of concerns.

Information regarding the student can be gathered from a variety of sources, including existing records that describe the student's current performance in school, along with the effects of the school experience on the student outside school. Current grades are reflective of performance, as are teacher reports, family observations, and the student's assessment of concern about herself of himself. In addition, valuable information may be gleaned from attendance records, aptitude or achievement tests, teacher recommendations, anecdotal reports, discipline reports, medical records, parent information, and any formal or informal testing. For schools using portfolio assessments, the student's portfolio can be a rich source of information. A careful review of the portfolio can reveal insight (along with documentation) into the student's struggles with the instructional process.

Andy's parents contributed significantly to the evaluation process through their observations and recording of their concerns. In their talks with the consultant, they shared their concern and provided a detailed history of Andy's struggles with school. Andy's medical diagnosis of ADHD and his history with Ritalin also contributed significant information to the evaluation process through showing a history of difficulties with the attending and learning strategies necessary for a successful classroom experience.

In our experiences with Section 504 plans, we have obtained information from a wide array of people: grandparents and other relatives; siblings; neighbors; scout leaders; coaches; friends of the student; custodians; foster families; cafeteria workers; school office staff; school nurses; school counselors; drama, art, and music teachers; and after school care workers, to name a few. In addition to gathering information from people, we also look at materials produced by or about the student. Besides student portfolios, information sources include report cards, teacher–parent communication notebooks, current test scores, recent assessment results, cumulative records, medical records, and reports from other professionals or agencies having contact with the student. Whenever possible, we attempt to review student work: written reports, tape-recorded oral reports, math papers, science projects, social studies projects, assignment notebooks, language arts lessons, and videotapes of the student engaged in instructional activities.

Developing the Section 504 Plan

Developing a Section 504 plan is the responsibility of the group of people knowledgeable about the student, the evaluation process, and placement or educational options under Section 504—in other words, the same people who performed the evaluation of the student for whom the plan is being written. The 504 committee or team determines whether the referred student is eligible for Section 504 protection, and, if so, carries out the evaluation, design of a 504 plan, and the periodic reevaluations required by Section 504.

Identifying Resources

Developing a Section 504 plan for a student becomes easier once resources for implementing the plan are identified. For instance, prior to the evaluation and design of a plan for Andy, the district consultant provided Andy's teachers with materials and information related to Section 504, and she met with the teachers and Andy's parents to familiarize them with their rights and responsibilities under Section 504. Andy's teacher, Diane, said of the process:

> When the consultant first met with us [the teaching team] and said we were going to work together to develop a 504 plan for Andy, I didn't know what she was talking about. She had been to our classrooms and observed Andy, and she had interviewed us about what our impressions were of Andy, including what we were concerned about, as well as what we saw as Andy's strengths. Before we started working with her, I only thought of Andy as a problem. His parents were trying very hard to help him, and I knew they were concerned, but we just didn't know what to do—any of us. The consultant brought us materials to read that suggested many different strategies we might try. She asked us to review the materials and meet together on our own (without her, the parents, or the administration) to discuss the suggestions and brainstorm modifications and strategies we all felt comfortable trying. Since we are organized into teaching teams with a common prep period, it was easy to meet.
>
> Then she met with us again, without the parents or principal, to discuss our ideas. I know she also met with Andy's parents during this time. She also recommended Andy's parents see a neuropsychologist for an evaluation. No one discussed putting Andy in special education. We didn't feel that was appropriate for him and, besides, we are a full-inclusion school, so his placement would not have changed.
>
> After a few weeks of working with the consultant, I really wanted to try the 504 plan. I was interested in learning about a new way to help kids, and I was feeling comfortable with the process. Andy was already doing better because we were seeing him in a different way. Everyone was a little more relaxed, and several of us on the teaching team began trying some of the ideas we were discussing even before we met to develop the plan. (Newbill, 1997)

Diane's comments make clear how critical resources are to the development of a successful 504 plan. Perhaps the most valuable resource was the district consultant, whose knowledge about Section 504 and her availability to the process were responsible for the process beginning at all. In addition, the materials supplied by the consultant gave all four teachers new knowledge, not only about Section 504, but also about how to modify their teaching to help Andy. Because the teachers share a common preparation period, they were able to discuss their ideas as a team. And Diane points out that meeting without the parents or administrators prior to the formal evaluation and implementation meeting was valuable for the team because they could be learners, and they had a bit of time to discuss what they were learning and how they might apply it.

One of the most highly valued resources for classroom teachers is time. Although Andy's teachers share a common planning time, many classroom teachers' schedules do not allow for collaboration. The building administrator can greatly facilitate the development of a 504 plan by creating times for various sorts of planning and preparation, such as including time for teachers to meet together to share strategies that might help the student, or for in-class observations by consulting and/or support teachers to assist the general classroom teacher in designing modifications for the student.

Communication While Developing the 504 Plan

As with most processes that depend on multiple participants, clear communication is an essential ingredient. When Andy's family and his teachers agreed to use his assignment notebook as a means for communicating between home and school, the probability that his 504 plan would succeed improved considerably. In addition, Andy's teachers' discussions of possible modifications and accommodations expedited the actual development and implementation of the plan that emerged as most likely to succeed.

For other students, lack of communication among those responsible for implementing the plan has resulted in the plan's failure and the student's subsequent loss of the support necessary for successful participation in the classroom. One such example is what happened with Jeffrey, who was an eighth grader in middle school when he was referred for a Section 504 plan by a pediatric neuropsychologist who was reevaluating Jeffrey at his parent's request. Jeffrey had been diagnosed with ADHD in the second grade, and medication had been prescribed. Jeffrey's parents stopped giving him the medication almost immediately because they were unhappy with the undesirable side effects. Jeffrey had difficulties in school throughout his elementary years and had attended a private, Christian school for a time.

In fifth grade Jeffrey returned to public school, where he was described as quiet and passive during class. Jeffrey frequently lost his work or failed to turn it in for a grade. Jeffrey's teachers reported that his parents expected them to "fix" the situation, while Jeffrey's parents felt the school was doing nothing to help him succeed.

Once Jeffrey entered middle school, his parents continued their complaints, and Jeffrey's teachers and the school counselor reported that the parents never followed through with their part of any agreements that had been made—e.g., to check Jeffrey's assignment notebook daily. Meanwhile, Jeffrey had developed some powerful avoidance techniques and took almost no responsibility for his own learning.

During the reevaluation the neuropsychologist recommended a trial of medication, which the parents refused. They also refused a psychoeducational evaluation to see if Jeffrey qualified for special education services, and they refused individual or family counseling. However, when a Section 504 plan was recommended, Jeffrey's parents agreed, although Jeffrey declined to attend the meeting to discuss what modifications would be implemented.

Jeffrey's 504 plan included an agreement that his teachers would give him extra time to complete work, give credit for partial work completed, and accept late work for up to a week after the due date. As part of the plan, Jeffrey was required to have his assignment notebook initialed by each teacher after he recorded any assignments (classwork or homework) that needed to be completed, as well as the due date. Jeffrey's parents agreed to check his assignment notebook daily.

During the first two weeks of the plan, Jeffrey "lost" his assignment notebook. Neither his parents nor his teachers made efforts to communicate with each other about the "lost" notebook. At a follow-up meeting, it became clear that no one—including Jeffrey—was invested in making the situation better, in spite of Jeffrey's parents' fears and concerns about his transition into high school the next year. The poor communication among those involved in developing the 504 plan resulted in the failure of the plan that had been developed for Jeffrey.

Another aspect of communication surrounding Section 504 plans concerns the written documentation required for compliance, a topic we discuss in depth in Chapter 4, where we show a sampling of the policies and procedures that districts have developed for Section 504. For now, though, we can say that the formatting and length of any documents associated with the 504 plan can make or break the plan. Long, complicated-looking documents with an abundance of text appear formidable, especially to families for whom this may be a first contact with their child's school. Well-designed and carefully thought-out forms can serve the purpose of clear, concise communication, while at the same time they can provide the documentation necessary to show the essential elements of the plan.

Implementing the Section 504 Plan

The implementation phase of the Section 504 plan occurs after the student has been identified and referred for the 504 process and the evaluation has taken place. Implementation typically takes the form of modifications and accommodations that are designed to enable the student to participate in and benefit from the school experience. In Chapter 3 we return to a specific discussion of modifications and accommodations. For now, we turn our attention to who is responsible for implementation and to the resources and support necessary for successful implementation.

Who Is Responsible for Implementation?

Each student's unique disability and educational needs will dictate who is responsible for implementing the 504 plan. In many cases, primary responsibility rests with the student's classroom teachers. In Andy's situation, all of his core teachers shared some responsibility, as did his parents. In addition, over time, Andy himself came to bear some of the responsibility.

For other students, however, implementation falls to different people. We mentioned earlier a situation in which a 504 plan called for the student's parents and the school nurse to review the student's medical records related to juvenile arthritis. In another instance, the 504 plan for Joanne, who has a seizure disorder, indicated that one of the primary implementers would be her tennis coach. The plan was constructed so that the coach would be responsible for speaking regularly by phone with Joanne's doctor, who would advise the coach about the best way to schedule and manage Joanne's practice time and tournament matches to minimize the effects of heat, fluid loss, and exertion.

Another example is that of Jeremy, an eighth grader who had been hospitalized for an acute episode of depression, including a suicide attempt, following the sudden death of his mother. Afraid that his classmates would stare at him like he was a "freak," Jeremy was reluctant to return to school. Though he had always earned good grades and wanted to continue learning more about photography, his greatest interest, following his hospitalization Jeremy was having difficulty concentrating and remembering daily assignments.

The district educational consultant received the referral for Jeremy's transition back to school. She arranged to meet with Jeremy and his family and arranged with the school counselor for a few support sessions in a small group with some of Jeremy's closest friends. During the sessions his friends told him how much they missed him and how they wanted to help him feel comfortable at school. When the 504 plan was developed, the team arranged for time twice a week during the lunch period for Jeremy's support group to eat together in the counseling center. In addition, with the consultant's facilitation, the teaching team agreed to prioritize Jeremy's assignments to delete those not considered central to the curriculum.

In addition, the team decided to give him more time to complete assignments. The team agreed to meet before the end of the term to see how Jeremy was doing and to determine if an alternative grading system might be needed. Finally, the plan included a system whereby Jeremy would check either with a peer or the teacher to make sure he had his assignments.

In Jeremy's plan, shown in Figure 2.3, different people were responsible for various components of the plan. The consultant assumed responsibility for initiating the 504 planning process; the school counselor arranged the support sessions; Jeremy's teachers devised modifications to assist Jeremy's transition back into the classroom; and Jeremy's friends participated through their support of his return, and through their roles in helping him make sure he had his assignments.

Resources and Support

In our earlier discussion of resources in the section titled "Developing the Section 504 Plan," we focused on the importance of the district consultant, who provided to Andy's teachers materials and information about the Section 504 process. We also talked about

(*text continues on page 45*)

Section 504 Plan

Lynda Miller, Ph.D.   Chris Newbill, Ph.D.

I. REFERRAL DOCUMENTATION

1. General Information

Student Name __Jeremy__ Birth Date __6/12/84__ Today's Date __4/6/96__

Address _____ City _____ State _____ Zip _____

Parent(s) Name(s) _____ Home Phone _____ Work Phone _____

504 Coordinator _____ Phone _____

2. Referral

1. Is there a disability/handicap present that substantially limits one or more major life activities?

    Yes ☒ No ☐ If yes, which major life activity is limited? (check one or more, as appropriate)

    ☐ caring for self   ☐ walking   ☐ seeing

    ☐ hearing   ☐ speaking   ☐ breathing

    ☒ learning   ☐ working   ☐ other (describe) _____

2. Describe the nature of the concern. __Jeremy has recently been released from the hospital following an acute episode of depression. His parents report he has been depressed.__

3. Describe how the disability/handicap affects a major life activity. __Jeremy has missed a considerable amount of school, and his worry about how his friends view him is affecting his ability to learn.__

4. Evaluation required? Yes ☒ No ☐ Date __4/6/96__ Signed __site Section 504 coord.__
   (person(s) making referral)

    If yes, schedule a Section 504 evaluation meeting and provide the following items to the parent(s)/guardian(s).

	Date sent	Sent by
• Notice of Section 504 meeting	4/5/96	(Team leader)
• Parent/student rights under Section 504	4/5/96	(Team leader)
• Acknowledgment of receipt of above forms (and parent response to scheduled meeting)	4/12/96	

    Date of Evaluation Meeting: __10/2/96__ Time of Meeting: __7:45 a.m.__

    Location of Meeting: __L Middle School__

    Reason for Meeting: ☒ Initial Evaluation

    ☐ Periodic Reevaluation

    ☐ Reevaluation before significant change in placement

(continues)

Figure 2.3. Jeremy's Section 504 plan.

II. EVALUATION AND ELIGIBILITY DOCUMENTATION

1. **Review of Available Information** (include test scores when appropriate)

   1. Summarize present levels of performance in areas evaluated. _Jeremy's last grades before he was hospitalized were above average. However, he has missed several weeks of school._

   2. Teacher reports/comments: _The counselor in Jeremy's school has talked with some of his friends, who have agreed to some support sessions with Jeremy before he returns to the classroom. His teachers are willing to make modifications in grading and assignment loads._

   3. Areas of concern: _The primary area of concern is Jeremy's anxiety and the work he has missed because of the hospitalization._

   4. Health and development: _Jeremy is suffering from depression and will be followed as an outpatient for 3 months after he returns to school. Otherwise, his health is unremarkable._

   5. Further information needed? Yes ☐ No ☒
      a) If yes, what information is needed?
         _NA_

      b) Person responsible for obtaining information: _____
      c) Date, time, and place to reconvene committee: _____

   6. Evaluation was conducted by: (list names)
      (Jeremy's parents; his teachers; the school counselor; site-based 504 coordinator)
      _____
      _____
      _____
      _____

2. **Eligibility**

   1. Does the student have a limiting mental or physical condition? Yes ☒ No ☐
      If yes, which major life activity is limited? (see p. 1 for list of conditions) _learning_

   2. Rank the severity of the impairment.

	Mild				Severe
	1	2	3	4	⑤

   3. Rank the duration of the impairment.

	Short				Long
	1	②	3	4	5

Figure 2.3. Continued.

3. Placement

      ☒ regular classes   ☐ regular classes AND accommodative services

      ☐ special education   ☐ special education AND accommodative services

4. Date, Time, and Location of
**   Accommodation Plan Meeting:** <u>10/3/96</u>   <u>7:45 a.m.</u>   <u>L. Middle School</u>

                                         Date   Time   Location

III. SPECIFIC ACCOMMODATIONS NEEDED

1. Describe the specific accommodations planned for this student, including the person responsible for each.

Accommodations Needed	Responsible Party
(1) Adjust assignments to decrease workload.	(1) All teachers.
(2) Provide a peer support group two times/week.	(2) Counselor.
(3) Give Jeremy extra time to complete assignments.	(3) All teachers.

2. Criteria to be used to evaluate the accommodation plan: <u>Teacher anecdotal reports and grades.</u>

3. Person(s) responsible for evaluating the accommodation plan: <u>Teachers and counselor.</u>

Figure 2.3. Continued.

SPECIFIC ACCOMMODATIONS (Cont'd)

4. Participants—the persons whose signatures appear below developed this accommodation plan:

Name	Title	Date
Mr. Williams	Parent	(dated)
Mr. Hobby	English	(dated)
Mr. Robinson	Math	(dated)
Mrs. Currey	Social Studies	(dated)
Ms. Scarborough	Science	(dated)
Ms. Chelsea	School 504 Officer	(dated)

5. Date for accommodation plan review/reassessment: 12/2/96

6. Person(s) responsible for accommodation plan review/reassessment: All teachers & counselor

7. Parent statements:

[X] I received a written notice of my rights under Section 504.

[X] I received notice of the Section 504 evaluation meeting.

[X] I received notice of the Section 504 accommodation plan meeting.

[X] I agree with the Section 504 plan as it is written.

[X] I understand that, if I disagree with the content of this plan, I have the right to ask for a Section 504 review meeting or impartial hearing by filing a written request with the district Section 504 coordinator.

(signed & dated)
_____
Parent/guardian signature   Date

_____
Parent/guardian signature   Date

ADDITIONAL NOTES

_____
_____
_____
_____
_____
_____
_____

Figure 2.3. Continued.

the importance to teachers of time for collaboration, observations, and discussions regarding strategies for students.

In addition to those related to support and/or consultative personnel and to time, some valuable resources are materials, policies and procedures, community, inservice, and peers.

Support and/or Consultative Personnel

Some districts are redefining the concept of student service delivery in an effort to provide classroom teachers with a support team. That is, resource room teachers or consulting teachers, instead of spending 100% of their time providing direct services to students, are reassigned for part of their day to serve on a school support team. The purpose of the team is to offer classroom teachers a forum for discussing students they find challenging or difficult, exploring new instructional strategies, developing classroom research projects, or asking for guidance on a particular issue or concern.

Materials

For some students, the Section 504 plan might include a provision for a set of textbooks the student can use at home. Or a plan might include purchasing outlines of textbook chapters or using volunteers to make the outlines. Study guides can be developed and reproduced for students who need them. Some students' plans may require reading materials at various reading levels or the use of taped materials. Increasingly, materials are becoming available on disk or CD-ROM for use on the computer. Schools that have been adopted by businesses, agencies, or individuals can often obtain free materials from their sponsors, and some companies offer materials to schools for projects related to their companies' products or to programs sponsored by their companies.

Policies and Procedures

Every teacher is aware of the increasing demands of paperwork. Section 504 is no exception regarding documentation. However, districts can decrease the paper glut and render more efficient the entire process of evaluating, implementing, and documenting Section 504 plans by developing streamlined policies and procedures. Of course, districts will want to make certain that the 504 policies and procedures they develop are comprehensive and legally solid. Nevertheless, the language used and the formatting chosen will have a dramatic impact on the understandability and efficiency of the 504 process. Our point is that clear, succinct, readable, understandable documents act as a resource, while long, legalistic, complicated documents usually result in more work.

Community

Some schools and classrooms have received resources of various sorts from an assortment of community agencies, individuals, and groups, including museums, botanical gardens, park and recreation districts, state or national parks, physicians, newspapers, radio and television stations, police and fire departments, and state or federal agencies, as well as businesses, as mentioned in the Materials section above.

In some instances, classroom teachers have sought assistance from community sources for a particular student because of a Section 504 plan; in others, teachers have requested services for an entire classroom or group of classrooms. Our aim here is simply to make readers aware of the vast resources available in their communities.

Inservice

District inservices can be used to train teachers in the use of a variety of instructional strategies, especially those pertinent to the modifications and accommodations required in Section 504 plans. For example, teachers can learn to use a method called the "guided lecture," in which the teacher provides partial outlines of his or her lectures. As the teacher presents new information, the students complete the lecture outline, comparing notes with partners or with the teacher as the lecture continues.

District inservices can also be used to familiarize teachers with examples of the types of Section 504 plans that have been developed for the district's students. Teachers could learn how to document their 504 activities, and they could practice designing 504 plans for hypothetical students. We return to this topic in Chapter 5, where we present an in-depth discussion of inservice presentations on Section 504.

Peer Support

In Jeremy's 504 plan, his peers played a vital role. They provided him with much-needed support at a time when he was feeling shaky about himself and anxious about returning to school. In addition, they offered a valuable service in helping him make certain he got his class assignments.

Another instance involves Yolanda, a fourth-grade student whose family's home burned. Yolanda's school is organized around teaching teams; she belongs to a fourth- and fifth-grade team that uses the Tribes approach developed by Jeanne Gibbs (1994). Following the Tribes method, students work in groups of various sizes for a good part of each school day. Immediately following the fire, Yolanda's teachers initiated the development of a 504 plan for her. The first step was to determine whether Yolanda met the requirement of a physical or mental impairment that substantially affected a major life activity. The six teachers and the school counselor on the team agreed that Yolanda's performance in school was seriously affected by her experience, and a 504 plan was designed. The most significant aspect of her plan was to reduce her responsibilities to her work groups so that she would not feel overwhelmed. A highly responsible group member, Yolanda had demonstrated anguish at letting her group down on the project they were working on at the time of the fire.

In addition to the reduction of responsibility to her group, the plan included time for her group to meet with the school counselor to discuss the fire, its effects on Yolanda and her family, and the expected course of her recovery. The plan also specified time for at least one community meeting (of the combined fourth- and fifth-grade students in her class) for Yolanda's teachers—and Yolanda herself, if she wished—to answer questions about the fire and for her classmates to demonstrate support for Yolanda in whatever manner they chose. Figure 2.4 shows Yolanda's 504 plan.

Reviewing and Evaluating the Section 504 Plan

Section 504 requires periodic reevaluations of all students for whom 504 plans have been developed and implemented. Although the statute is not specific regarding a timetable (unless a significant change in placement is considered), most districts follow the IDEA schedule for reevaluations, which is at least every three years. Students for whom the 504 committee recommends a significant change in placement—other than for disciplinary reasons—must be reevaluated prior to the change. Many districts also have a policy that the student's 504 committee may reevaluate at their discretion or if reevaluation is requested by one of the student's teachers. In addition, the 504 committee may stipulate a series of periodic reviews of the 504 plan in order to catch any problems as they arise and to modify the plan as the student's experiences dictate.

Collecting Data

Collecting data to document a 504 plan can take a variety of forms. The most typical criteria used are grades, anecdotal reports from teachers and parents, assignment notebooks, agenda books, student anecdotal reports, material from a student's portfolio, in-class test results, attendance, tardiness, and number of disciplinary incidents. In general, the data used to document the accomplishment of a student's 504 plan will originate most often from the student's teachers, although parents and family members will often provide critical information as well.

Our experience has been that the easier it is to collect the data, the more likely it is to be collected. If possible, data collection should be planned as part of what already happens in the student's school day, e.g., through notations in an assignment notebook, anecdotal notes taken during scheduled observations, signatures on homework assignments, or attendance records tallied by office staff. Some teachers use "sticky" notes to collect anecdotal information and later stick them to pages in the student's assignment notebook or copy them to send home for a signature, while keeping the originals in the student's portfolio.

Evaluating Outcomes

As we have pointed out throughout this book, we view Section 504 as a formalized description of what good teaching should provide. As teachers we have a commitment

(*text continues on page 52*)

Section 504 Plan

Lynda Miller, Ph.D.   Chris Newbill, Ph.D.

I. REFERRAL DOCUMENTATION

1. General Information

Student Name _Yolanda_ _____ Birth Date _7/15/86_ Today's Date _4/5/96_

Address _____ City _____ State ____ Zip _____

Parent(s) Name(s) _____ Home Phone _____ Work Phone _____

504 Coordinator _____ Phone _____

2. Referral

1. Is there a disability/handicap present that substantially limits one or more major life activities?

   Yes [X]   No [ ]   If yes, which major life activity is limited? (check one or more, as appropriate)

[ ] caring for self	[ ] walking	[ ] seeing
[ ] hearing	[ ] speaking	[ ] breathing
[X] learning	[ ] working	[ ] other (describe) _____

2. Describe the nature of the concern. _Yolanda's performance in school has suffered following a fire that burned her family's house._

3. Describe how the disability/handicap affects a major life activity. _According to teacher observation and grades, Yolanda's learning abilities have been affected._

4. Evaluation required? Yes [X] No [ ] Date _4/5/96_ Signed _(school counselor)_
   (person(s) making referral)

   If yes, schedule a Section 504 evaluation meeting and provide the following items to the parent(s)/guardian(s).

	Date sent	Sent by
• Notice of Section 504 meeting	_4/5/96_	_(team leader)_
• Parent/student rights under Section 504	_4/5/96_	_(team leader)_
• Acknowledgment of receipt of above forms (and parent response to scheduled meeting)	_4/6/96_	

Date of Evaluation Meeting: _4/15/96_ _____ Time of Meeting: _8:40 a.m._

Location of Meeting: _A.C. Elementary School_

Reason for Meeting: [X] Initial Evaluation

[ ] Periodic Reevaluation

[ ] Reevaluation before significant change in placement

(continues)

Figure 2.4. Yolanda's Section 504 plan.

II. EVALUATION AND ELIGIBILITY DOCUMENTATION

1. Review of Available Information (include test scores when appropriate)

1. Summarize present levels of performance in areas evaluated. Following the fire that burned her family's home, Yolanda's performance in school has dropped significantly. Her grades have fallen, and she has not added to her portfolio since her return.

2. Teacher reports/comments: Yolanda's teachers are very concerned about her learning. She definitely needs support to help her through this transition. They have also noted that Yolanda has expressed considerable distress at letting her group down.

3. Areas of concern: Group participation with her tribe; project completion and portfolio development. All content areas.

4. Health and development: Not applicable

5. Further information needed? Yes ☐ No ☒

   a) If yes, what information is needed?
      NA

   b) Person responsible for obtaining information: _____

   c) Date, time, and place to reconvene committee: _____

6. Evaluation was conducted by: (list names)
   (Yolanda's parents; teaching team; school counselor)

2. Eligibility

1. Does the student have a limiting mental or physical condition? Yes ☒   No ☐

   If yes, which major life activity is limited? (see p. 1 for list of conditions) learning

2. Rank the severity of the impairment.

Mild			Severe	
1	2	3	④	5

3. Rank the duration of the impairment.

Short			Long	
①	2	3	4	5

Figure 2.4. Continued.

3. Placement

    ☒ regular classes   ☐ regular classes AND accommodative services

    ☐ special education   ☐ special education AND accommodative services

4. Date, Time, and Location of
Accommodation Plan Meeting: _4/6/96_   _8:10 a.m._   _A.C. Elementary School_
                                  Date   Time   Location

III. SPECIFIC ACCOMMODATIONS NEEDED

1. Describe the specific accommodations planned for this student, including the person responsible for each.

Accommodations Needed	Responsible Party
(1) Provide community meeting(s) for Yolanda's Tribe.	(1) School counselor
(2) Reduce her responsibilities to her Tribe.	(2) Teaching team
(3) Reduce her workload, especially the number of assignments and the components of portfolio projects.	(3) Teaching team

2. Criteria to be used to evaluate the accommodation plan: _Teacher observations; grades; portfolio._

3. Person(s) responsible for evaluating the accommodation plan: _Teaching team & counselor_

Figure 2.4. Continued.

SPECIFIC ACCOMMODATIONS (Cont'd)

4. Participants—the persons whose signatures appear below developed this accommodation plan:

Name	Title	Date
Mr. & Mrs. Gonzalez	Parents	4/6/96
Mr. Johns	Team teacher	4/6/96
Ms. Simmons	Team teacher	4/6/96
Mr. Riviera	Team teacher	4/6/96
Ms. Peterson	Team teacher	4/6/96
Mr. England	Counselor	4/6/96
Ms. Santiago	Section 504 Officer	4/6/96

5. Date for accommodation plan review/reassessment: 5/5/96

6. Person(s) responsible for accommodation plan review/reassessment: Teaching team & counselor

7. Parent statements:

   ☒ I received a written notice of my rights under Section 504.

   ☒ I received notice of the Section 504 evaluation meeting.

   ☒ I received notice of the Section 504 accommodation plan meeting.

   ☒ I agree with the Section 504 plan as it is written.

   ☒ I understand that, if I disagree with the content of this plan, I have the right to ask for a Section 504 review meeting or impartial hearing by filing a written request with the district Section 504 coordinator.

(signed and dated by parents)
_____
Parent/guardian signature   Date

_____
Parent/guardian signature   Date

ADDITIONAL NOTES

_____
_____
_____
_____
_____
_____
_____
_____

Figure 2.4. Continued.

to look at every student as a unique learner possessing a singular set of attentional, communicative, and experiential preferences. To the extent that we can match instruction to what is relevant and meaningful to our students' lives, we increase our chances of succeeding in our instructional mission. Section 504 offers us a means for formalizing the individualization of instruction and for evaluating its effectiveness.

One way we approach evaluating instruction—Section 504 plan or not—is to use the Reflection Checklist shown below. This checklist may help school personnel in evaluating whether their practices are consistent with a vision of caring. Items that are not currently consistent with your school's beliefs and practices can be used as the basis for discussion among your staff. Viewed in this context, a caring school is not characterized by a particular set of practices as much as by the commitment of its staff to continually develop its capacity to accommodate the full range of human differences among its learners as the school community moves toward a fuller realization of the ethic of caring.

A Reflection Checklist for Your School

☐ Do we genuinely start from the premise that each child belongs in the classroom that she or he would naturally attend?

☐ Do we individualize the instructional program for all the children regardless of differences or special needs and provide the resources that each child needs to explore individual interests and strengths in the school and community environment?

☐ Are we fully committed to the maintenance of a caring community that fosters mutual respect and support among staff, parents, and students?

☐ Does our administration contribute to the creation of a work climate in which staff are supported as they provide assistance to each other (or are teachers afraid of being presumed incompetent if they seek peer collaboration in working with students)?

☐ Do general and special educators integrate their efforts and resources so they work together as a team?

☐ Do we, as a school community, deal with our own problems in a way that models caring and mutual respect for our children?

☐ Are we prepared to alter support systems for students as their needs change throughout the school year so that they can achieve, experience success, and feel that they genuinely belong in their school and classes?

☐ Do we actively encourage and support the full participation of all children in the life of the school, including cocurricular and extracurricular activities?

The critical piece regarding the evaluation of the 504 plan is for those responsible for the plan to review the data in order to determine whether the plan is proceeding as conceived and specifically to focus on whether the plan is reducing and/or eliminating discrimination on the basis of the student's handicap. If the answer is yes, the committee can schedule another review, for the same purpose, in a reasonable amount of time. If the answer is no, further and/or different modifications must be devised and implemented as quickly as possible.

Student and Family Satisfaction

Section 504 is specific in its stipulations regarding student and family rights. If a parent or guardian disagrees with the student's Section 504 committee's decisions at any step of the process—identification, evaluation, or educational placement of their child—they may appeal the decision(s) before an impartial hearing officer. In addition, parents or guardians have the right to participate in the hearing and to be represented by counsel. Further, if the family disagrees with the hearing officer, they have a right to a review by a court of appropriate jurisdiction.

However, as we emphasized earlier, it is in everyone's best interests to initiate and maintain clear communication between the 504 committee, the student's teachers, the student, and the student's family. We have described at least one instance in which the student's family and teachers failed to communicate, with the result that the student's 504 plan failed as well. In Chapter 4 we return to this topic through discussion of the development of 504 policies and procedures.

Teacher Satisfaction

Our experience makes clear that if the teachers who will be implementing the 504 plan are dissatisfied, the plan itself had better be modified, or the planning process had better be altered to attend to those dissatisfactions. Without committed participation from teachers, the 504 plan will fail. We have found that several factors play a significant role in teacher satisfaction (recall Andy's teacher's comments in the section on identifying resources as part of developing the 504 plan).

One factor is that teachers need to be given the opportunity to learn about Section 504 and how they can use it before they are expected to develop and implement a plan for a student. They need information, materials, and someone to use as a resource for their questions.

Second, the committee should design a 504 plan that begins with the least number of modifications necessary for the student to begin to achieve success. We made the point earlier that trying to provide too many modifications at once may overwhelm both student and teachers. An analysis of the student's strengths and needs will clarify what already works, which can be used as a platform on which to build other modifications, a few at a time. Evaluating what is working in the plan requires that the number of modifications be kept small in order to understand which variable is contributing to which outcome.

A third factor is that if they are to be the implementors, teachers need to be full participants in the process of designing the plan. If the 504 plan is focused on the student's classroom or on the instructional strategies used, the student's classroom teachers are crucial players in the process of designing modifications and accommodations. Without their input the 504 plan cannot be appropriate for the student if it involves instruction.

A fourth factor involves the data collection process. As we noted above, the 504 committee, which should include the student's teachers if instruction is involved, must devise data collection strategies that are inherent in what already transpires in the classroom. To ask teachers to do more paperwork in their day is to risk derailing the plan.

Fifth, when student behaviors are the focus of the 504 plan, classroom teachers may need support in the classroom in order to implement the necessary accommodations—particularly if a teacher views the student as a problem. In our own experience as teachers, we have found that when we see students as problems, most often we do not know what to do to fully engage them in the instructional process. When we acquire the knowledge and/or skill to change our relationships with those "problem" students, our perceptions of them change significantly.

Modifying the Plan

Occasionally the 504 plan will need to be modified, particularly if it works better or faster than the committee thought it would when the plan was designed. The purpose of the periodic review of the plan is to ensure that modifications can be made as needed, rather than discovering too late that changes were indicated.

During reviews of the 504 plan, the committee—and the student, if possible and appropriate—can analyze the data that have been gathered, along with the evaluations that have been made of the accomplishments of the plan. Based on their findings, the committee has several options. If the disabling condition was temporary and no longer exists, the plan can be terminated if it is determined that the student needs no follow-up or transitional services. If the disability is not temporary and the plan is working well, the committee can continue the plan as is and schedule the next review.

If the disability is not temporary and the plan needs to be changed in any way, the committee can make the appropriate changes. If a significant change in placement is recommended, the student's family must be notified in writing; if the family is in attendance at the 504 committee meeting, the recommendation will most likely be a collaborative decision, and the notification can be performed during the meeting.

During 504 plan review sessions, instructional modifications will likely seem apparent and obvious because of certain pieces of information: the data collected about the modifications used to date, particularly teachers' notes and observations about effectiveness; and/or the evaluation of the accomplishment of the plan to date.

Summary

In this chapter we have discussed the Section 504 process, beginning with factors to consider before the plan is developed. We described the 504 evaluation process by a group of people knowledgeable about the student, about evaluation procedures, and about placement options; we included discussion of what to include in the 504 evaluation. In sharing our experiences about developing the 504 plan, we emphasized how to obtain the information necessary for developing a cogent plan, how to identify the resources that best support the plan, and the importance of clear communication among the 504 committee members, the student, and the student's family.

We ended the chapter by relating information about implementing 504 plans, as well as factors to consider in evaluating and modifying them. We concluded with a section on documenting the 504 plan.

Types of Modifications and Accommodations in a Section 504 Plan

Chapter 3

In Chapter 1 we discussed modifications within the context of our responsibilities to students under Section 504. In that discussion we listed several factors to consider when developing modifications for any student. Our purpose in presenting these criteria was to emphasize the relevance of the plan to the student's strengths and needs, as well as the reasonableness and parsimony of the accommodations from the teachers' perspective.

In this chapter we again consider modifications and accommodations, this time from the standpoint of which types to use under varying sets of circumstances. Because the design and implementation of effective 504 accommodations are crucial to the student's success in school, we offer here a variety of approaches and examples. In addition, we include several ways of approaching modifications because we know that readers bring different organizational preferences and can learn from a range of models, and we know that good teachers appreciate being able to construct what works for them from among many choices.

We believe that the most important component of the Section 504 plan is how effectively the planned modifications are designed and described so that they have the greatest probability of increasing the student's opportunities for success. In our experience, the most successful plans have resulted when teachers, the student (when appropriate), the student's parents/family, and school administrators work together to identify and describe the modifications to be implemented. In general, as we stated in Chapter 1, during the modificaton planning process we follow these guidelines:

- Focus on the student's strengths.
- Design the least intrusive intervention.
- Customize the modifications to fit the student's classroom setup.
- Consider academic modifications first.
- Match the modifications to the student's strengths and needs.
- Prioritize and implement only a few modifications at a time.
- Review and adjust accommodations continuously.

The next four sections of this chapter describe different models for approaching the design and implementation of modifications and accommodations for students under a Section 504 plan. In the fifth section we present our own approach and provide examples of accommodations taken from plans we have devised for students we know.

The CASE Approach

While the general guidelines we offered at the beginning of this chapter form the basis for designing modifications, there are several factors to consider when determining what accommodations to make for any given student. For instance, CASE describes four types of modifications that can be made under a Section 504 plan.

Modifications in Communication

Accommodations in communication between the student, the student's family, and the student's teacher(s) may take the form of a daily/weekly journal, periodic parent–teacher meetings, providing parents with sets of duplicate texts, or developing some form of parent/student/school contacts. Modifications in communication between school and community agencies, as long as parent/family consent is obtained, could be the identification and communication with the appropriate agency personnel working with the student, assistance in agency referrals, or the provision of appropriate carryover in the school environment. Modifications in staff communication might include identifying resource staff, networking with other staff, scheduling teambuilding meetings, or maintaining ongoing communication with the building principal (Council for Administrators of Special Education, 1992).

Modifications in Organization and/or Management

According to CASE, modifying organization and/or management might provide for modifying the student's instructional day, including allowing the student more time to pass in the hallways or modifying the student's class schedule. Another organizational/management accommodation is modifying classroom organization and/or structure by, for example, adjusting the student's placement in the classroom (e.g., using a study carrel or placing the student nearer the teacher), increasing or decreasing the student's opportunity for movement within the classroom. Modifying the district's policies or procedures by, for example, increasing the number of excused absences for health reasons, adjusting transportation or parking arrangements, or approving early dismissal for outside appointments, can also be helpful (Council for Administrators of Special Education, 1992).

Accommodations in Teaching Strategies

Examples of modifications in teaching strategies include designing alternative teaching methods, such as adjusting testing procedures (e.g., length of time allotted for the testing, administering the test orally, having the student tape-record the answers), individualizing the student's classroom and/or homework assignments, or utilizing technology such as computers, tape recorders, and calculators. Materials can be modified through using legible materials and materials that address the student's learning style or adjusting the reading level of materials (Council for Administrators of Special Education, 1992).

Accommodations in Classrooms and/or Buildings

If a student has a health condition, modifying the classroom or building climate might include use of an air purifier in the classroom, controlling the temperature, or accommodating specific allergic reactions. If a student requires accommodations that include equipment such as a wheelchair or crutches, the plan could include provisions for evacuation or a schedule in accessible areas. Students with special dietary or medication needs could be accommodated through modifications in building health or safety procedures (Council for Administrators of Special Education, 1992).

An Example from an ADHD Program

Doudy et al. provide a comprehensive description of classroom accommodations in their discussion of the needs of students with ADHD (1997). Although their approach is focused on a specific group of students, their perspective encompasses any student for whom a 504 plan is being considered. In their discussion Doudy et al. consider four types of accommodations: curricular content, instructional materials, instructional practices, and assignments given to and products required from students.

Curricular Content Accommodations

Doudy et al. (1992) remind us that 504 plans focus not just on the stated curriculum; they also take into account aspects of the student's experience that lie outside what is formally mandated in the explicitly stated curriculum. That is, a Section 504 plan can also focus on the hidden curriculum, in other words, what teachers actually teach through inferences about the explicit curriculum and through informal conversations and references; and on the absent curriculum, what is not taught because it has been excluded for some reason (Doudy et al., 1992). According to Doudy et al., examples of 504 plan accommodations lying outside the explicit curriculum are study skills that support the efficient and effective acquisition, recording, remembering, and using of information; learning strategies, including learning how to learn, analyze, and solve problems; social skills such as learning what is socially acceptable and what is not; and related life skills such as daily living, recreation and leisure, community participation and citizenship; transportation; and health.

Accommodations in Instructional Materials

Instructional materials encompass a wide range, including texts, overhead transparencies, audio- and videotapes, maps, globes, photographs, drawings, newspapers, magazines, worksheets, workbooks, weekly periodicals, basals, formulas, schematics, computer-generated images, filmstrips, and commercial materials. In designing modifications under 504 plans, accommodations may address any combination of these materials.

Modifying Textual Material

Doudy et al. (1997) offer three types of textual modifications: adapting textual material, enhancing student comprehension, and helping students retain information they have acquired through text.

Text can be adapted through such means as providing audiotapes, reading material aloud, pairing students for mastery of text-based material, delivering the information through another means, working individually with students or in small groups, using a multilevel, multimaterial approach, developing abridged versions of text-based content, or simplifying existing textual material (Doudy et al., 1997).

Doudy et al. (1997) propose several approaches for enhancing student comprehension, including

- providing students with a purpose for reading what they are required to read,
- previewing any reading assignment,
- teaching students to use format features of text,
- stimulating the student's interest prior to reading,
- using a study guide,
- using graphic organizers,
- modifying the reading assignment (e.g., length or pace),
- highlighting text, and
- teaching comprehension-monitoring strategies.

To assist students in retaining what they have read, Doudy et al. (1997) suggest using graphic aids, incorporating formal learning strategies, teaching test-preparation skills, and teaching class-discussion preparation skills.

Adapting Nontext Materials

Polloway and Patton (1997) emphasize several factors to consider when creating accommodations of nontextual materials, specifically math materials and what they call learning aids. They suggest that modifications focus on designing specific teaching strategies for teaching a particular skill; providing sufficient practice time; slowing the pacing in moving the student from one skill or topic to another; reviewing previously covered material; translating the language carrying the math information or the concepts conveyed; offering a wide variety of types of activities for each topic or skill; making certain the activities and content are relevant to the student; making certain students possess appropriate skills for working in cooperative groups; and providing natural, in other words, noncontrived, problem-solving applications.

Selecting Commercially Available Materials

If a Section 504 plan is devised that requires the acquisition of a commercial product, several questions should be considered in evaluating the appropriateness of the product for any particular student:

- Is the material appropriate as is?
- Would the material be appropriate with modification?
- If yes, what type of modification would be required?
- Does the organization of the material allow for the evaluation required in this student's 504 plan?

Modifying Instructional Practices

Good teaching underlies all modification of instructional practice. As Doudy et al. (1997) point out, good teachers use a combination of teacher-directed, student-directed, and peer-directed teaching. Good teachers understand that different students possess different ways of learning, retaining, and understanding information, each of which requires a different approach to instruction.

According to Doudy et al. (1997), good teachers practice the basic elements of effective teaching through

- staying close to students who are experiencing learning-related problems;
- demonstrating what is to be learned, giving the student an opportunity to try out the behavior or skill with support from the teacher, and having the student practice without assistance;
- using a multisensory approach;
- modifying their lectures in a variety of ways; and
- using assistive technology.

Assignment and Products Accommodations

Teachers' expectations of the products students produce range from completed homework assignments to independent research projects. Good classroom teachers offer their students a variety of product options, often in the context of portfolio assessment. Doudy et al. (1997) provide a comprehensive list of product ideas for teachers considering accommodations for a student whose 504 plan requires adaptation in products (p. 130).

In making modifications in assignments, teachers can shorten assignments, break them into parts, change what constitutes successful completion, allow additional time for completion, reduce the difficulty of the content, or change the output mode (Doudy et al., 1997). Similarly, homework adaptations could include participation of the parents/family in monitoring homework; modifying how homework is managed by the student, teachers, and family; and adapting homework assignments to fit the student's strengths.

An Example from a Behavioral/ Learning Approach

Hoover and Patton's (1997) comprehensive description of curricular adaptations for students with learning and behavioral problems offers another valuable approach to the design of modifications for students under a Section 504 plan. Hoover and Patton's adaptations fall into four categories: general adaptation guidelines, adaptation strategies, cooperative learning, and technology.

Their first three general adaptation guidelines, which are similar to those of Doudy et al. (1997), address adaptions in curricular content, instructional strategies, and instructional settings. In a departure from the approach taken by Doudy et al., Hoover and Patton include the modification of student behaviors as a fourth general curricular adaptation. They emphasize that students' management of their own behaviors is frequently related directly to classroom instructional settings, instructional strategies, and the type of content to be learned. Thus, they indicate that modifying student behaviors must be seen within the context of instruction, rather than viewed in isolation or as separate from classroom settings and events. In our discussion of our own approach to modifications for students' 504 plans, we will return to the topic of student behaviors.

Hoover and Patton (1997) describe three types of adaptation strategies that can be used to meet students' learning needs: teaching strategies, student learning strategies, and student study strategies. In their discussion of teaching strategies that can be used to accommodate a student's learning needs, they present 21 strategies, each with a brief description, major advantage(s), example(s), suggested uses, and special considerations for general education settings. For example, here is one of the 21 teaching strategies, "Providing Choices":

Description
  The learner is given two or more options from which to select in order to complete an assignment.

Advantages
  This strategy may assist in reducing fears associated with various assignments or types of tasks or may alleviate problems associated with teacher-student power struggles.

Examples

Offer two different math papers, both of which address the same objective you wish the student to meet. Allow the learner to select and complete one of the papers for the assignment.

Suggested Uses

Giving students choices within structured situations helps them to become more responsible for their own education.

Inclusive Considerations

The teacher should ensure that the student knows exactly what the choices are and that he or she will be held accountable for whatever choice is made. (Hoover & Patton, 1997)

Hoover and Patton (1997) follow a similar format in describing 6 student learning strategies and 23 student study strategies that can be used to accommodate students' needs. In addition, the authors provide a helpful table showing each of the student learning strategies, the key elements involved, and the curriculum areas affected and another table showing each of the study strategies, the relevant task areas covered by each, the process involved, and classroom applications.

Cooperative Learning

Much has been written on cooperative learning, particularly in the 1990s. Hoover and Patton (1997) include discussion of cooperative learning as a means for accommodating students' learning needs and emphasize the research showing the effectiveness of cooperative learning for students with learning problems who are placed in inclusive settings. We are in agreement with Hoover and Patton that cooperative learning can be an effective and powerful approach for many students needing accommodation under Section 504. They write, "Cooperative learning has been found to be effective in various subject areas with a variety of students who possess varying skill levels. It is a teaching practice that facilitates effective implementation and adaptation of curricula in special and inclusive class settings. The implementation of cooperative learning may involve a variety of groupings or pairs with an emphasis on different content areas or behavior skills" (1997). In addition, Johnson and Johnson (1990) indicate that cooperative learning helps students in several areas of learning: learning basic facts, understanding concepts, learning to solve problems, and using higher-level thinking skills.

Technology

In their presentation of classroom adaptations for students, Hoover and Patton (1997) include discussion of recent technological advances such as computers, computer-based expert technology, electronic communications, and distance learning. To this list we would add Internet technology and software, which afford students access to an immense network of data and information. Hoover and Patton include descriptions of various computer technologies, including some that help educators identify appropriate assessment and intervention methods and instruments, some that provide curricular adaptations for students with learning and behavioral problems, and some geared for students to learn content, behavior, and learning skills.

Sample Modification Strategies from a School District

Many districts have developed comprehensive modification strategies for use in planning individual students' Section 504 plans. One with which we are familiar comes from the Gallup–McKinley County School District in New Mexico, which has formulated a well-thought-out Section 504 policies and procedures handbook (Gallup–McKinley County School District, 1996). This handbook contains a set of sample strategies and classroom and homework modifications for what the district terms the Individual Accommodation Plan (IAP), or the Section 504 analogue to the IEP required under IDEA.

The sample IAP strategies suggested in the Gallup–McKinley County policies and procedures handbook (Gallup-McKinley County School District, 1996) are organized into nine categories, each of which includes a detailed list of examples. The nine categories are:

- physical arrangement of room,
- lesson presentation,
- assignments/worksheets,
- test taking,
- organization,
- behaviors,
- mobility,
- pacing, and
- social interaction supports.

Modifications to the Regular Education Curriculum

The Gallup–McKinley County Schools handbook (1996) describes numerous modifications that can be used in the regular education classroom to accommodate students with disabilities. Examples include giving open-book tests, underlining or highlighting the major points in an assignment, providing cue cards and spelling lists, permitting students to tape responses to assignments, and grading for content rather than mechanics or spelling.

Modifications in Homework

The Gallup–McKinley County Schools handbook (1996) suggests several modifications that teachers and parents can use with students needing support for completion of homework and assignments. The suggestions include setting an agreement with the student's teacher(s) regarding the maximum and minimum amounts of homework per night, helping the student prioritize assignments, providing the student with a study guide to help prepare for tests, and using flash cards, tape recordings, or short quizzes to help the student prepare for major tests.

A Comprehensive Approach to Modifications

The approaches we have presented in the two preceding sections arose from the work of special educators whose primary concerns were ADHD (Doudy et al.) and learning and/or behavior problems (Hoover & Patton). Our own thinking about modifications for students has arisen from numerous sources, including both regular and special education. We have also borrowed promising ideas from the literature, and we have talked with hundreds of teachers throughout the United States and Canada about their experiences in devising accommodations to fit students' learning strengths and needs.

Our efforts have focused on designing solutions for students and/or teachers with problems or concerns. Among others, we've attempted to assist students whose preferred modes of learning were not recognized by their teachers, students whose cultural and/or behavioral patterns were perceived as threatening, and students whose families could not provide them the support they needed to succeed in school. We have offered our help to teachers who have desired to better serve their students, to teachers who have resisted all efforts to bring change, and to teachers who wanted to initiate change but were not sure how to proceed.

As we mentioned earlier, we use a set of guidelines in planning and implementing modifications for Section 504 plans. These guidelines rest on a set of assumptions we make about everyone, regardless of age, gender, race, ethnicity, cultural makeup, socioeconomic status, or geographic region:

- Everyone is capable of learning.
- Everyone is smart; our job is to find out how, not how much.
- Everyone is smart in multiple ways.
- Everyone shows a unique pattern of strengths.
- Individual variation is a gift, not a disorder.
- Everyone possesses preferred ways of attending.
- Everyone presents a unique pattern of learning.
- A deficit/disorder does not describe a person; it describes a condition the person has.
- Test scores tell a very small part of each person's story.

Using these assumptions, we have developed a methodology for describing learners and designing instruction, which we have described in previous publications (Miller, 1991, 1992, 1993a, 1993b; Miller & Miller, 1994, 1996; Miller & Newbill, 1992). What is pertinent to our topic in this book is that to design instruction of any type—mandated or modified—requires a commitment to the *student's* perspective. You will see in our discussion in this section that our primary concern is to inventory the student's strengths, ascertain the student's educational needs, and design instruction that facilitates the student's learning in the most efficacious, efficient way.

Typical Modifications for the General Education Classroom

A good place to start in thinking about modifications is to look at some examples of typical modifications for the general education classroom. We organize these general accommodations into three categories: academic, behavioral, and physical. The following is a list of these modifications, along with descriptions of typical accommodations we might use for each.

Academic Modifications

1. Communication and teaching methods

   - Devise quiet cues, that is, agreed-upon signals between the teacher and student (e.g., teacher taps finger on forehead to mean, "You can take a water break now").
   - Use verbal signals (e.g., "This is the main point. Write it down in your notes").
   - Redirect (e.g., "Point to number 4").
   - Give short, concrete directions (e.g., "First, read the paragraph. Second, underline all the verbs").
   - Use examples (e.g., calling on different students to work examples on the board until everyone understands the process).
   - Prompt students to repeat directions in their own words.
   - Use eye contact and proximity to the student.

2. Expectations

   - Give a clear statement of expectations, using a written rubric whenever possible.
   - Use a timer so students can try to beat their own time.
   - Assist students in helping one another in a natural way.
   - Use pass/fail evaluation on some assignments.
   - Break up long assignments into steps, with a review after each step.
   - Design individualized classroom/homework assignments.

3. Setting demands and the environment

   - Allow more or less movement as needed.
   - Provide appropriate seating (e.g., students have seat heights that allow their feet to rest flat on the floor and that space them appropriately for the task at hand).

- Use a variety of evaluation techniques (e.g., written tests, oral responses, demonstration of knowledge).
- Use a consistent routine for transitions (e.g., starting class the same way every day with a brief orientation exercise).
- Offer peer support (e.g., study partners, or pre-quiz partners before a test).
- Use an alternative grading system.
- Allow more time between classes.

4. Materials

- Provide two sets of books, one for use at home on homework.
- Highlight texts.
- Provide study guides or outlines of texts.
- Provide guided outlines that students fill in as the teacher lectures.
- Use materials that are legible for the student (e.g., large print).
- Adjust reading levels of materials.
- Use technology (e.g., computers, recorded materials).

5. Follow-up

- Check for understanding frequently throughout the lesson.
- Send daily/weekly reports home.
- Send home a monthly schedule of tests and long-term assignments.
- Pair up all students with a phone-study buddy.
- Schedule team meetings at regular intervals.

Behavioral Modifications

1. Rules and consequences

- Require the use of an assigment notebook.
- Use individual contracts that clearly state rewards and consequences.
- Reward achievement with the students' preferred activities.
- Clearly state and review rules with the class.

2. Behavioral management

- Give choices whenever possible.
- Recognize any effort or progress toward compliance.
- Work together to distinguish deliberate noncompliance from inability.
- Accept gradual approximations to desired behavior.
- Help children rehearse socially acceptable responses.
- Enlist parents as partners both in recognizing positive behavior and in using consequences for negative behaviors (e.g., in designing daily/weekly reports).
- Never use humiliation to control behavior.
- Never discuss specific students' behavior problems in public (e.g., in the teacher's lounge).

Physical Modifications

1. Equipment

   - Provide appropriate furniture and equipment (e.g., pencil tripod, footstool).
   - Provide access to technology (e.g., computer, calculator, reader).
   - Provide alternative curricular materials (e.g., consumable math text).

2. Classroom/building

   - Use an air purifier in the classroom.
   - Control the room temperature and humidity.
   - Accommodate specific allergic reactions.
   - Develop an evacuation plan for students in wheelchairs or using crutches.

3. Health

   - Use a health management plan.
   - Administer medication.
   - Accommodate special diets. (Newbill, 1997)

As you can see from the list, most of the accommodations we have included seem to follow common sense. These are modifications good teachers make regularly, almost without thinking about them. However, in the context of developing modifications as part of a Section 504 plan, the alterations planned for any particular student must be specified and documented.

Teaching Modes and Teaching Techniques

In addition to considering typical modifications that might be made in a general education setting, we have found it helpful to consider the various teaching modes and the specific teaching techniques required for each. Wood (1992), in addressing how to teach at-risk students in general education classrooms, presents a clear organizational scheme for these modes and their associated techniques. She identifies four teaching modes: the expository mode, or providing an explanation; the inquiry mode, or assisting students in answering a guiding question or hypothesis; the demonstration mode, or providing experiences for students to watch or attend; and the activity mode, or providing actual experiences for students to learn by doing. Table 3.1 shows the specific techniques used in each of the four modes.

For each of these four modes, Wood also offers a set of alterations or modifications for students in need. For instance, in describing alternative teaching techniques for lecturing within the expository mode, Wood suggests providing lecture outlines, providing a copy of lecture notes, and using transparencies to provide a visual presentation simultaneously with the lecture (Wood, 1992, p. 229). Examples of the alternative teaching techniques Wood offers for self-directed study within the inquiry mode are giving specific directions about what to do; making directions short, simple, and

Table 3.1
Teaching Modes and Specific Techniques

Expository Mode	Inquiry Mode	Demonstration Mode	Activity Mode
Lecture	Asking questions	Experiments	Role-playing
Telling	Stating hypotheses	Exhibits	Constructing
Sound filmstrip	Coming to conclusions	Simulations	Preparing exhibits
Explanation	Interpreting	Games	Dramatizing
Panels	Classifying	Modeling	Processing
Recitation	Self-directed study	Field trips	Group work
Audio recording	Testing hypotheses		
Motion pictures	Observing		
Discussion	Synthesizing		

Note. From *Adapting Instruction for Mainstreamed and At-Risk Students* (2nd ed.), by J. W. Wood, 1992, New York: Macmillan. Copyright 1992 by Macmillan. Reprinted with permission.

few; and collecting and placing resources for study in one area (p. 236). For examples of using games within the demonstration mode, Wood recommends designing games in which the acquisition of skills, not winning, is the priority, making directions simple, highlighting important directions with color codes, working with peer tutors, letting students prepare their own games, and designing games that emphasize skills needed by the students (p. 241). Finally, for using dramatizing within the activity mode, Wood suggests respecting the privacy of those who do not want parts and letting such students help others prepare sets (p. 242).

Modifications for Some Common Situations

In our work designing Section 504 plans for students, we have encountered students with some common situations, such as behavioral and emotional concerns; anxiety and/or depression; loss of motivation; problems with handwriting, written language, reading, or math; and difficulty in completing in-class work or homework. In this section, we share with you some of the adaptations we have found to work best in these situations.

Behavioral and Emotional Concerns

Students experiencing a behavioral or emotional problem frequently have weak or inconsistent "inner voices," leading them to manipulate others because of their reduced ability to control or manage their behaviors internally. What disturbed and disturbing children require from adults is thinking responses, not feeling or emotional ones.

Teachers, administrators, and parents must think deeply and set into motion the structures that provide predictable psychological safety for these students.

When disturbed children enter an environment with no clear boundaries or too-rigid boundaries, they frequently experience increased stress; the emotions these children show under such circumstances are usually anger or deep hostility. Anger may show as active or passive aggression, acting out of control, or withdrawal—all efforts to block adults and to express deep fear and/or inadequacy. Most of us first respond to such behavior with empathy, which typically does not elicit the response we expect. When we are confronted with more anger or hostility, we usually shift into a "high control" mode, and we find ourselves in a showdown with the student.

Our challenge as teachers in these circumstances is how to address the needs and general welfare of the class as a whole, while at the same time managing individual variances and needs. What renders security and safety for disturbed children is to know that the adult (teacher) is in charge, has established clear rules providing for the physical and psychological safety of the classroom, will respond specifically and directly about misbehavior, and will not respond to argument or manipulation.

Unless schools are prepared ahead of time, crises can develop in which everyone loses. For example, if a student with a behavioral disability refuses to do anything and the teacher requests or threatens some aggressive action, the likely result will be the student's hitting, pushing, throwing objects, or running away. In our experience, crises can be averted through several means.

First, a school can develop a schoolwide crisis intervention plan in which the entire staff is trained to implement the plan in a collaborative way. The plan should include a common signal for assistance over the intercom that brings *immediate* assistance. As part of the plan, all the adults in the school should know how to help if there is a fight threatened or in progress. Second, the school can provide a conflict mediation program that includes teaching students how to solve their own problems and that rewards nonviolent and collaborative conflict resolution. Third, each classroom can develop a crisis intervention plan, which will most likely require the assistance of a behavior management specialist. The classroom plan can then be discussed with each class when teachers review rules and consequences.

Section 504 plans for students with behavior disabilities can include modifications for teachers' use during threatened crises. An example from our work is David, a 15-year-old boy with a temper. David has expressed that when he feels angry and a teacher moves in closer to him or raises his or her voice, he feels threatened, and teachers have reported that David typically strikes out or grabs something to throw when this occurs. The modifications below, developed by all of David's teachers and with input from David and his mother, centered on Mr. Hansen, as he reported experiencing more conflicts with David than any of his other teachers. David's 504 plan included these modifications:

1. When David loses his temper, Mr. Hansen will lower his voice and move physically away from David.

2. Mr. Hansen will recognize that David is angry through saying, for example, "I see that you are feeling angry," not "I understand."

3. Mr. Hansen will offer David choices so that he will feel he has some control of the situation—for example, "You can sit in the back and take a break, or you can go to Ms. Phillips's room for a few minutes. I will give you a pass."

4. Mr. Hansen will offer to drop the issue (and really drop it) that caused the confrontation for now—until a later time at which both can discuss it objectively, saying something like, "We can talk this over later when we're both feeling calmer."

5. Mr. Hansen will provide every means for David to save face.

6. Mr. Hansen and David will hold a private conference later to resolve the conflict. Mr. Hansen will enforce reasonable consequences and ask David to commit to trying another way of resolving a conflict when he begins to feel angry.

7. Mr. Hansen and David will devise a quiet signal that David can use to signal that he needs a break before he becomes so angry he cannot control his behavior.

8. Mr. Hansen will praise David's efforts to interrupt his cycle of temper tantrums.

9. Mr. Hansen will model ways to respond to stressful situations.

10. Mr. Hansen will incorporate relaxation activities throughout his class periods.

11. Mr. Hansen will hold class meetings that focus on how to cope with powerful feelings in difficult situations.

The modifications devised for David focused primarily on altering his environment so that he perceived it as safer and less threatening. Over a 16-week period, during which Mr. Hansen received the support of his building administrators and his fellow teachers, David's outbursts in Mr. Hansen's class decreased from at least one per day (David saw Mr. Hansen for two periods each day) to four episodes over the entire 16 weeks. Another effect of this particular 504 plan was that Mr. Hansen reported feeling much less irritated by David and more valued by him as someone who could offer something important.

Sadness, Anxiety, and Depression

A surprisingly large number of students exhibit anxiety, sadness, and depression at school, with causes ranging from family matters to chronic school failure. These feelings make it difficult for students to concentrate or exert effort in school, which, in turn, leads to school failure (or *more* school failure) and anxiety. If depression is suspected, family members must be encouraged to seek professional help. In any case, children exhibiting these feelings need sensitive care and understanding from parents and teachers, especially as many children do not recognize fully what they are feeling and that it can be changed.

The suggestions we offer here are intended as a general guide for use in planning modifications for students experiencing sadness, anxiety, and/or depression:

- Many anxious children improve dramatically when they feel school is a safe place. To make classes as emotionally safe as possible, avoid causing embarrassment by using criticism or by calling attention to the child (e.g., by sending the child to sit in the hallway, where she or he can be seen by all passersby).

- Children who display anxiety, sadness, or depression in school may need direct help with their academic self-esteem. Teachers should look for roles or activities in which the student feels confident or can gain status. False praise should be carefully avoided (e.g., praising a student for doing things that anyone can do or does). Instead, recognize improved effort or attempts at learning.

- Students can be given jobs that increase social status—for example, for younger students, helping to organize a bookshelf or run an errand; for older students, becoming an older-buddy reader or math partner for a younger student.

- When school-related anxiety is clearly identified—for example, fears of being beaten by other students or fear of humiliation in physical education—teachers and administrators should intervene directly. The matter should be discussed privately with the student, and if the anxiety is great, some negotiating can take place to reduce the fear. Just as adults take steps to avoid unpleasant or embarrassing situations, we can help students do the same.

- Children who are sad, anxious, or depressed need to know that there is at least one person in school in whom they can confide their concerns—teacher, counselor, adviser, or administrator. Whoever the student confides in should avoid preaching, be a good listener, and act as an advocate for the student.

We participated in developing a 504 plan for a fifth-grade girl, Lisa, whose teacher had requested assistance for Lisa because of her recent withdrawal and drop in performance in class. When the school counselor contacted Lisa's parents, they were relieved to learn that the school was concerned enough to try to intervene with Lisa. The parents related that, over the past six weeks, Lisa had become withdrawn and sad; they had tried to discover the reason for her behavior but had not identified anything that could be causing her distress.

At the 504 planning meeting, attended by Lisa's teacher, her mother and father, the school counselor, and the district behavior specialist, the team recommended a series of interventions, beginning with the school counselor, whom Lisa had talked with the previous year following her grandmother's death:

1. Ms. Jarratt will meet with Lisa three or four times over the next two-week period to see if she can determine why Lisa's behavior has changed so dramatically.

2. The 504 planning team will reconvene in three weeks to review progress to that date.

When the team reconvened following Ms. Jarratt's meetings with Lisa, we learned that Lisa had confided in her about a situation in which some older boys were sexually harassing her (Lisa had agreed that Ms. Jarratt could relate her story to the team). She had been afraid to tell anyone for fear they would carry out their threats. Once she knew that Ms. Jarratt was concerned about her behavior, she realized she didn't have to remain quiet any longer.

Because the school administration took immediate steps to resolve the problem with the boys who had been harassing Lisa, Lisa's behavior returned to what it had been before her experiences with the boys. The 504 team agreed to meet in two months to review the situation, which showed that Lisa was maintaining her original school behavior. As a corollary, the boys and their families were provided with counseling over a 4-month period as a condition to their continued attendance in the school Lisa attended. In addition, the four boys involved agreed to participate in a community-service program at a local day-care facility associated with a battered women's shelter.

Motivational Loss

Because school is a powerful influence on students' motivation, we must understand the possible reasons for a student's loss in motivation. The greatest contributors we have found are persistent failure in school or outside, poor grades, and problems at home or with friends. We have found that placing the blame for lost motivation with the student does not solve the problem. Rather, an analysis of what leads to a student's experiencing success provides the key to understanding what motivates that student. To this end, we teachers can do the following:

- Program successful experiences for students, which often means allowing students to show competency through, for instance, oral testing or demonstrating their skills and knowledge.

- Show compassion and caring for students, including encouraging any attempts the student makes to improve his or her school performance. What this means, also, is that we must take care not to criticize students with low motivation in front of others or tell them such things as, "You could do better if you wanted to."

- Find out what the student's strengths are and enlist these in reengaging the student in school. Even simple responsibilities can help restore interest and motivation. For example, a student who is a good artist might be invited to illustrate classroom materials or teach the class how to draw something specific.

- Reduce, prioritize, or restructure the workload for students who are feeling overwhelmed by school demands and who feel it is impossible to meet current expectations.

- Discuss with the school counselor (or another appropriate person) the possibility of a student being depressed and, if appropriate, recommend the family for professional services.

- Look for other ways students can demonstrate competency. For instance, cooperative learning or peer test-taking groups give students opportunities to team up with peers of varying strengths and weaknesses.

In a fourth- and fifth-grade combined classroom in the school in which we work, the two-teacher team responsible for the classroom had been concerned about Joanie since school had begun 6 weeks before. She had seemed unmotivated to participate in any of the classroom activities, and she had turned in only a few of the assignments thus far. The teachers knew that Joanie was capable of above-grade-level work, but their efforts so far had not seemed to engage her interest. In this particular school an individual learning plan, similar to a Section 504 plan, is developed for every student, not just those with disabilities. Joanie's two core teachers met with their team, which included two other two-teacher teams for fourth and fifth graders, the assistant principal, and a classroom learning consultant, to formulate a plan to rekindle Joanie's interest in learning.

As part of the curriculum, the entire fourth–fifth-grade team incorporates both multiple intelligences, or MI theory (Gardner, 1993), and the Tribes (Gibbs, 1994) philosophy of teaching. Thus, Joanie's 504 plan consisted of two steps: first, assessing Joanie's preferred modes of attending and learning based on MI, along with observing her preferred modes of interaction with classmates during the Tribes activities; second, designing activities and learning experiences based on the results of step one.

What the team learned was that, from both the MI perspective and the Tribes observations, Joanie's preferred approach to learning seemed to be through interaction with others, including teachers and peers. At the request of her parents, for the first six weeks of classes, Joanie had been working primarily by herself rather than in a cooperative group, or Tribe. Once the team had performed its assessment of Joanie's learning preferences, it approached her parents with the recommendation that Joanie be assigned to a Tribe for the bulk of her learning day. Based on the team's observations and analyses, the parents agreed. At the learning review scheduled 6 weeks after Joanie's assignment to a Tribe, the team noted marked changes in Joanie's participation and interest, and her grades had improved significantly. Most important, Joanie acted happier at school, and her parents were pleased with her performance.

Alternative Grading System

We have recommended alternative grading systems for a large number of students for whom we have written Section 504 plans. While some teachers use portfolios or projects upon which to base students' grades, most continue to use the traditional grading system whereby students are compared with each other and assigned a letter or numerical grade based on their performance on tests. For some students, however, the traditional grading system may not be appropriate. For them, test scores, class participation, and behavior might be weighted differently, or one of the following might be used.

- *Student self-comparison.* Individual students meet with their teachers to determine appropriate instructional goals within the curriculum and to keep track of the student's progress toward those goals. That progress, rather than a comparison with the student's peers, is then reported on the report card.

- *Contract grading.* Individual students and teachers determine the amount and quality of the work the student must complete to receive a specific grade. Contracts should include content to be mastered, activities, specific product, resources to be used, and how the student will demonstrate mastery.

- *Pass/fail system.* Minimum passing course competencies are specified. If the student demonstrates mastery of these minimum competencies, she or he receives a P grade; failing to meet the minimums results in an F grade.

- *Mastery level/criterion system.* Teachers divide materials into a hierarchy of skills and activities, based on individual needs and abilities as measured by a pretest. After completing learning activities, the student takes a posttest (not necessariliy written) or performs an activity or activities to demonstrate mastery of the content. Students receive credit for the content or skill(s) and move on to the next one.

- *Checklists.* Teachers develop checklists that delineate competencies associated with their courses and evaluate individual students by identifying which competencies have been mastered.

- *Multiple grading.* Teachers give multiple grades based on ability, effort, and achievement. The ability grade is based on the student's expected improvement in content areas. The effort grade is a measure of time and energy invested by the student. The achievement grade assesses the student's mastery of the content in relation to peers.

- *Level grading.* Teachers individualize the grading system by using a subscript to indicate the level of difficulty at which the student's grades are based. For example, a grade of "B_4" can be used to note that a student is working in the B range at the fourth-grade level.

- *Descriptive grading.* Teachers write descriptive or narrative comments and give examples regarding the student's performance, which provides parents, students, and other educators with information regarding the student's skills, learning style, effort, and attitude.

Handwriting

Handwriting, the motor production of legible written language with appropriate speed, is often a problem for students diagnosed as having a learning disablity or ADHD. Poor handwriting may be part of a larger motor dysfunction that includes inability to coordinate the muscles of the hand and forearm, or it may be part of problem with short-term memory function. Because writing requires holding in active short-term memory both the mechanics of writing (letter formation, spelling, grammar, and punctuation) and composition, memory capacity may be exceeded by the multiple demands of writing. When combined with poor organization and language difficulities, writing may be the greatest challenge some students face in schoolwork.

Parents and teachers who are aware that students are having difficulty with handwriting must recognize that the students may be embarrassed and ashamed of writing. Here are some suggestions for supporting students with handwriting difficulty:

- Reduce the amount of written work required. Allow students to show work in other ways whenever possible.

- Allow more time for written tasks.

- Emphasize one skill at a time for a written task, such as content only, or spelling only, to reduce memory and attentional demands and to allow the student to focus on mastering one skill at a time. Allowing time for writing a rough draft that can be edited over time can be very useful.

- Provide breaks by alternating written tasks with activities that don't require writing.
- Allow students to find a way to sit that is comfortable for them.
- Provide soft rubber pencil grips to aid in positioning and grip.
- For some students, a mechanical pencil provides more feedback and makes writing easier.
- Teach keyboarding skills, and provide a student with a word processor to bypass the grapho-motor demands of writing.
- To reduce the possibility that students with writing problems will give up on writing entirely, focus on reducing the load of written demands.
- Support the student's efforts at writing, regardless of whether s/he uses manuscript or cursive. Encourage success however the student finds it.

In developing a Section 504 plan for Grant, a 13-year-old boy, we addressed hand-writing as one of our concerns. Grant had attended a private school throughout elementary school and was preparing to make the transition into a public middle school for seventh grade. His parents were concerned about the transition for several reasons, including that he was accustomed to individual and personal attention in his private school setting, he was a boy who enjoyed arguing with his teachers as part of the learning process, and his handwriting was severely impaired. His teacher in private school was committed to Grant's success in middle school.

The 504 planning team[1] consisted of Grant's current private school teacher, his parents, and a learning consultant. In the handwriting portion of his 504 plan, we formulated these accommodations for Grant:

1. Grant's parents would purchase a keyboarding program for Grant to learn on his home computer.

2. Grant's teacher would design alternative means for Grant to produce reports and essays, including making oral presentations, audiotaping of products, and dictation to a test-taking buddy.

3. Grant's teacher would provid time each day for Grant to practice his keyboarding on the classroom computer.

Grant's 504 plan will go with him to public school in the fall so that the 504 planning team there will be able to use it as a basis for developing a new one for his new situation.

---

[1]Even though Grant's private school receives no federal funding, and is therefore not required to comply with Section 504, it routinely uses Section 504 plans for its students as part of its commitment to nondiscrimination.

Completion of In-Class Work and Homework

In situations in which it is difficult to assess how much a student can do at a given time, it is helpful to set expectations at a reasonable level based on experience with that student. Then, if expectations are met or exceeded, the student can earn certain privileges. If the student does not meet expectations—for whatever reason—the privileges can be withheld. We strongly recommend that you *not* withhold regular daily events such as physical education, art, recess, music, or drama when a student's learning and/or emotional problems interfere with her or his ability to perform. And, except on rare occasions, adding work that has not been completed at school to a student's homework will increase the student's stress and anxiety level rather than result in more completed work.

We suggest helping students set up a simple system they can use to monitor their own progress regarding work completion. For instance, we have used a chart in a special folder so the student and teacher can initial a box for each task completed in each subject area. The student can then graph each day's rate of completion, which is a good way to look for behavioral or emotional patterns that might help identify problem times (e.g., Mondays, or afternoons).

Because some students need frequent breaks between difficult or challenging assignments, a contract can be used to specify water or bathroom breaks after a designated amount of time working on a specific task or activity. Sometimes a timer can be used to cue the student regarding work times and break times.

Seating choices can affect the amount of work a student completes. Some students need to move from a chair to the floor, or against a wall or cabinet, to improve completion efforts.

We view homework as the practice or reinforcement of concepts learned at school, and we believe that, for younger students, parents—not teachers—should be the monitors. As older students begin to assume responsibility for their own homework completion, some, especially those with learning difficulties, will require a 504 plan to provide assistance from the teacher to break up long-term assignments into clear, distinct steps to be completed by the student. The plan may also include having the teacher devise an outline for the student to use in identifying the steps of the assignment.

For younger students, the 504 plan may stipulate that the student's teachers and parents determine a reasonable amount of time for the student to work on homework each night (e.g., 30 minutes in grades 1–2; 45 minutes in grades 3–4; 1 hour in grades 5–6). After the student spends the agreed-upon time on homework, the child may receive privileges for work completion (e.g., watching TV, playing on the computer, a special dessert). If the work is not complete, the parent notifies the teacher and does not award the privileges. The important point here is to reward effort, but don't punish the inability to perform. Rather, withholding privileges provides the consequence for uncompleted work.

Older students should be part of the 504 planning process, which ensures that the accommodations are reasonable from the student's viewpoint. A 504 plan addressing completion of homework for an older student might include a reduced homework load compared with that of peers, a project individualized for the particular student, or alternative assignments suited to the student's learning strengths.

Written Language

Most teachers require students to respond to and demonstrate mastery of specific content by producing a written product. However, while many students can master the content of an assignment, their writing difficulties can interfere with their performance. It is common for students with writing problems to have more than one source of difficulty, including handwriting (described more thoroughly above), retrieval memory, organization, motor memory, and attention. In addition to constructing other means by which students can respond or demonstrate knowledge and skills (e.g., orally, by audiotape, artistically), teachers can support students' efforts in producing written products by:

- scheduling and audiotaping writing conferences with the student to clarify ideas, outline responses, and provide feedback;
- encouraging the student to use the dictionary, personal dictionary, and thesaurus;
- providing checkpoints during the assignment process to monitor the student's work;
- allowing the student to redo work for an improved grade by responding to the teacher's feedback;
- giving separate grades for content, spelling, and grammar, or focusing on only one of these areas per assignment or per stage of an assignment;
- breaking long-term writing assignments into steps to complete a writing assignment in stages, rather than trying to finish everything at the last minute, under "emergency" conditions;
- giving more time to complete written assignments or adjusting the amount of writing required to complete an assignment (e.g., copying spelling words 2 times instead of 5; writing 3 pages instead of 10); and
- modifying the evaluation phase to assess performance differently, perhaps based on effort or improvement rather than on a single external standard.

With Sol, a ninth grader whose written language output was historically sparse, the 504 planning process provided a simple solution by systematically reducing the amount of written language he was required to produce and increasing the amount of time he was allotted to produce. His plan also included learning keyboarding so that the demands of the task of writing itself would not decrease his output. His teachers determined that Sol could demonstrate his ability to produce both narratives and descriptive language by audio- or videotaping his responses to assignments.

Mathematics

A student's ability in mathematics draws from a number of functions, each of which must be well developed and integrated in the student: various aspects of memory, visual processing, abstract thinking, language ability, problem-solving skills, and the ability to put what has been learned to practical use. In addition, because math is highly cumulative, mastery of current concepts depends on what was learned previously. Many students develop "math anxiety" because they worry about their ability to perform and because learning mathematics can be emotionally charged.

Some strategies we have found to help support math learning include the following, any of which can be incorporated into a Section 504 plan.

For Parents

- Encourage and give positive feedback for hard work. Determine if your child understands the concepts in any given assignment; act as a resource for your child if your own math abilities permit.

- If you feel feel unsure of your ability to help your child with math, consider a math tutor. Ask your child's teacher about other teachers or students from a local college who could be hired at a reasonable fee or look for a math tutor for your child through a community agency or church.

- Provide your child with games (computer or other) that offer math practice.

- Emphasize how math is used in everyday life.

For Teachers

- Provide comprehensive programming that offers a wide range of math activities and skills, including, for younger students, computation, operations, word problems, mathematical reasoning, time measurement, fractions, and applications. For older students include mathematical systems, mastery of the various symbol systems, and applications.

- Individualize math programming by offering adaptations in both the task or activity as well as the way the task is learned. For example, some students learn math facts through rote drill, while others learn best by associating facts with other, known facts. We invite you to consider that individualizing does not necessarily mean students working alone. Rather, small groups of students working on the same problems and using similar strategies can work together, even if they have different levels of abilities.

- Provide correction and feedback as soon as possible. Showing students patterns in their efforts and teaching them to check their own work and monitor their own progress can make a major difference in sustaining the motivation and perseverance they need to progress in learning mathematics.

- Provide students access to a wide range of approaches to instruction. Despite years of research, no single method of teaching mathematics has been shown to be significantly better than others. Offering students access to a range of formats (e.g., textbooks, workbooks, math stations, manipulatives) increases the likelihood of their achieving success in learning math.

- Provide plenty of applications for students to see the real-world applicability of the concepts and skills they are learning. Concrete materials and real-life applications of math problems make math real and increase the probability that students will transfer their skills to applied settings at home and at work.

Reading

Children with reading difficulties are likely to experience breakdowns in one or more of the processes that underlie efficient reading, including word identification, phonological awareness, vocabulary, and overall language skills. When these processes are absent or underdeveloped, students experience a range of consequences, such as avoidance of reading, poor fluency, and inflexible reading style, among others. And if a student has any problems with attention or persistence, she or he may get discouraged easily and give up learning to read well.

While the discussion of learning to read is beyond the scope of this book, we can offer suggestions intended to help students experiencing reading difficulty, regardless of the exact nature or cause of the difficulty.

For Parents

- Establish an atmosphere that encourages reading. Until your child begins to read on his or her own, read aloud to him or her every day. The bulk of research shows that reading aloud to children is the single most effective support parents can use to strengthen their reading. Even 10 to 15 minutes of reading each day is enough to improve your child's vocabulary, comprehension, and motivation for reading. Choose something to read that you both will enjoy, and take a few minutes to discuss (no questioning!) what is happening in the story and what might happen next.

- Use reading as a family to discuss upcoming events, such as reading about a place you will visit, or to understand world events. Make sure your child sees how you use reading in your daily life, for instance, in reading the newspaper.

- Help your child find reading materials that focus on a strong interest, such as space or animals or computers. If your child wishes to read to you, keep the time short and pleasant; don't use the time for drill, teaching, or questioning.

For Teachers

- Establish a purpose for every reading assignment.

- Alternate direct teaching of reading skills with open reading for pleasure.

- Pair poor readers with a reading partner for SSR. Require them to read the material, not just talk or look at the pictures; this means one partner needs to know how to read.

- Recognize and encourage any gains for the child.

- Pair reading practice with strength areas, such as art or music.

- For students for whom the reading material is too difficult, use assistants, parents, or older students to tape-record reading material.

- Provide outlines or study guides and use advanced organizers to help students get ready to read. Introduce and discuss new vocabulary prior to reading.

- Give more time to complete reading tasks, or reduce reading amounts.

- Be sensitive to the embarrassment a student may feel on being asked to read aloud.

- Use a variety of supports, such as maps, graphs, and webs to support reading comprehension.

Summary

In this chapter we described various sorts of adaptations that can be used with students who are experiencing difficulties in learning in school. We began with a discussion of Doudy et al. (1997) and Hoover and Patton (1997), whose accommodations, while designed for students with ADHD and behavior and learning problems, respectively, provide valuable information for anyone participating in the Section 504 planning process.

The bulk of the chapter focused on the types of modifications that can be used with students with assorted kinds of learning problems. We suggested a variety of approaches, and we provided examples of the modifications used in the 504 plans of several students with whom we are familiar.

Policies and Procedures for Complying with Section 504

Thus far we have focused on defining and describing Section 504, identifying the processes associated with the statute, and discussing several different approaches to the modifications supported by 504 plans. In this chapter we approach the factors associated with compliance to Section 504. This chapter is not intended as an in-depth treatment regarding compliance. For that, we refer you to other sources, such as Smith and Patton (1998) or *Section 504 Compliance* (1997), both of which address the legal aspects of complying with Section 504.

Our intent in this chapter is to provide you with the information you need to include in a Section 504 policies and procedures handbook. We have drawn from numerous sources in the hope that we have included all pertinent material. Nevertheless, we realize it is impossible to include everything, and many states and districts have their own unique requirements regarding Section 504. Therefore, we invite you to use the information in this chapter with the knowledge that it may not include everything you will need to comply fully with your district's or state's Section 504 requirements. Appendix A contains examples of the various forms we mention throughout this chapter.

What To Include in a Section 504 Policies and Procedures Handbook

Introduction

The introduction of the policies and procedures handbook could begin with the district's statement regarding its prohibition of discrimination against anyone with a disability or impairment. Such a statement might read:

▶ *Section 504 and IDEA (the Individuals with Disabilities Education Act) are federal laws prohibiting discrimination against individuals with a disability or impairment by any program or activity receiving federal financial assistance. In order to fulfill its obligation under Section 504 and IDEA, the [your school district's name here] school district will not knowingly permit discrimination against any person with a disability or impairment in any of the programs and practices of the school district. The school district has the responsibility to identify, evaluate, and, if the child is determined to be eligible under Section 504, afford access to appropriate educational services.*

> *If the parent or guardian disagrees with the determination made by the professional
> staff of the school district, she or he has a right to use the mediation process and/or a hearing
> with an impartial hearing officer.*

Some districts include in the introduction a statement regarding parent/guardian
rights under the Family Educational Rights and Privacy Act of 1974 (FERPA). The
introduction section should also include a copy of what is included in the Section 504
statute—

> No otherwise qualified individual with handicaps in the United States shall, solely by rea-
> son of her or his handicap, as defined in section 706(8) of this title, be excluded from the
> participation in, be denied the benefits of, or be subjected to discrimination under any pro-
> gram or activity receiving or benefitting from federal financial assistance. {29 U.S.C. Sec.
> 794; 34 CFR 104.4 (a)}

— as well as the definition:

> [A]ny individual who has a physical or mental impairment (or has a record of such impair-
> ment), or is regarded as having such an impairment, which substantially limits one or more
> major life activities, such as caring for one's self, performing manual tasks, walking, seeing,
> hearing, speaking, breathing, learning, and working. {29 U.S.C. Sec. 706(8); 34 CFR
> 104.3 (j) (i), (ii), (iii)}

Because Section 504 is a statute related to discrimination against those with disabilities, a description of what constitutes discrimination under Section 504 can also
be included in the introduction. The statement below is used by CASE.

Discrimination under Section 504 occurs when a recipient of federal funds:

1. Denies a handicapped person the opportunity to participate in or benefit from an
   aid, benefit, or service which is afforded nonhandicapped students (e.g., district
   practice of refusing to allow any student on an IEP the opportunity to be on the
   honor roll; denial of credit to a student whose absenteeism is related to her/his
   handicapping condition; expelling a student for behavior related to her/his
   handicapping condition; refusing to dispense medication to a student who could
   not attend school otherwise).

2. Fails to afford the handicapped person an opportunity to participate in or benefit
   from the aid, benefit, or service that is equal to that afforded others (e.g., apply-
   ing a policy that conditions interscholastic sports eligibility on the student's
   receiving passing grades in five subjects without regard to the student's handicapping condition).

3. Fails to provide aids, benefits, or services to the handicapped person that are as
   effective as those provided to nonhandicappped persons (e.g., placing a student
   with a hearing impairment in the front row as opposed to providing her with an
   interpreter). Note: "Equally effective" means equivalent as opposed to identical.
   Moreover, to be equally effective, an aid, benefit or service need not produce
   equal results; it *must merely afford an equal opportunity to achieve equal results.*

4. Provides different or separate aids, benefits, or services unless such action is necessary to be as effective as the aides, benefits, or services provided to nonhandicapped students (e.g., segregating students in separate classes, schools, or facilities, unless necessary).

5. Aids or perpetuates discrimination by providing significant assistance to an agency, organization or person that discriminates on the basis of handicap (e.g., sponsoring a student organization that excludes persons with handicaps).

6. Denies a person with handicaps the opportunity to participate as a member of a planning or advisory board strictly because of her/his handicapping condition.

7. Otherwise limits the enjoyment of any right, privilege, advantage or opportunity enjoyed by other (e.g., prohibiting a person with a physical handicap from using a service dog at school).

8. In determining the site or location of a facility, makes selections which effectively exclude persons with handicaps, denies them the benefits of, or otherwise subjects them to discrimination (e.g., locating students with handicaps in trailers, wings in basements, or other unnecessarily restrictive classrooms). (Council of Administrators of Special Education, 1992)

Some districts include in the introduction a brief history of Section 504, similar to the information we used to begin Chapter 1.

Purpose

In a policies and procedures handbook, the purpose is typically stated early in the document. The purpose states that the representatives of the district, typically the school board, have approved and adopted the procedures described in the handbook. A sample purpose statement might read:

▶ *These procedures have been approved and adopted by (school district name) to comply with the preschool, elementary, and secondary education provisions of Section 504 of the Rehabilitation Act of 1973.*

Definitions

The handbook should contain a set of definitions to clarify the procedures. For instance, terms such as the following should be considered for inclusion:

- adult student
- disability
- handicap
- educational setting
- student with disability/handicap
- physical or mental impairment
- has a record of a physical or mental impairment

- is regarded as having a physical or mental impairment
- major life activity
- otherwise qualified
- Section 504
- Section 504 student
- student
- special programs
- free and appropriate public education
- eligibility

Eligibility and Referral

This section of the handbook should contain a description of the district's procedures regarding how students are identified and referred for a Section 504 evaluation. For example, the handbook could include the following questions, which form the basis for determining who is eligible under Section 504:

- Is the student's condition mental or physical?

- Does the student's condition *substantially* limit a major life activity; in other words, does it prevent equal access to a major life activity in the educational environment?

- Is the degree of the impairment significant?

- Does the student's condition require any accommodation in order to ensure the student's access to a free and appropriate public education?

The district's policy regarding student referral can be included in this section and may include a statement such as:

▶ *Any student who, because of a disability or perceived disability, needs or is believed to need special programs or related aids and services in order to receive an appropriate education, either academic or nonacademic, may be referred to the Section 504 designee by any person who has knowledge of the referred student's disability or suspected disability.*

The referral must be in the "Referral Documentation" section of the Section 504 Plan.

Most districts include in the handbook a form for documenting the referral, either as part of the evaluation process or as a freestanding document.

This section can also include the procedure the district follows upon receipt of a referral for a Section 504 evaluation, which could be something like the following:

▶ *Upon receipt of a referral for a Section 504 evaluation, the school site administrator or Section 504 designee shall take the following steps:*

- *Review and consult with persons knowledgeable about the area of concern to determine whether the Section 504 referral is appropriate. If the referral is not appropriate, notify the referring individual and document this decision on the Section 504 Referral Documentation Form. If the referral is appropriate, establish a Section 504 committee, set a* date for an evaluation meeting, and record the date, time, and location of this meeting on the Section 504 Referral Documentation Form.

- Prior to taking any action regarding the Section 504 evaluation, provide the following information to the parent(s)/guardian(s):

  - notice to parents of Section 504 evaluation, including date, time, and place of meeting (this could be a form duplicated ahead of time)

  - parent/student rights in identification, evaluation, and placement under Section 504 (this could be a form duplicated ahead of time)

  - acknowledgment of receipt by parent(s)/guardian(s) of above two pieces of information.

Evaluation

The evaluation process adopted by the district should be described in this section of the handbook. The section should include description of the Section 504 committee as well as what constitutes a Section 504 evaluation. A sample description including both components might read:

▶ *The Section 504 Committee established by the school-site administrator/designee shall be convened at the student's school of attendance. The Section 504 Committee will be comprised of the school-site administrator/designee, one or more other qualified persons knowledgeable about the evaluation process and placement or educational options available under Section 504, and one or more persons with knowledge about the student referred. Persons in this last member category may also have knowledge of the evaluation process and placement or educational options available under Section 504.*

It is the Committee's responsibility to gather and review data, to notify parents of the results of the evaluation, and to generate an agreed-upon Individual Accommodation Plan (IAP) for the referred student. In addition, the Committee has the responsibility to follow up with the teacher(s) to ensure that the IAP is being appropriately implemented and to schedule reevaluations as needed in each individual case.

All available information must be documented on the Section 504 Evaluation Documentation Form.

More specific information may be included to describe the district's procedures regarding the exact nature of what constitutes a Section 504 evaluation. For instance:

▶ *The Section 504 Committee will review and summarize current information and data from a variety of sources as the Committee deems necessary to make programmatic, placement, and accommodation decisions. These sources may include, but are not limited to, attendance records, aptitude and achievement tests, teacher recommendations, report cards, anecdotal records, discipline reports, parent information, medical records, physical condition, social and cultural background information, adaptive behavior, and informal or formal testing. The evaluation will consist of the informal collecting of existing information and data regarding the student referred. If the Section 504 Committee believes it is necessary, evaluation may also include formal testing of the student.*

If desired, the district can further specify what constitutes formal or informal testing, adaptive behavior, and specialized tests.

Individual Accommodation Plan (IAP)

The Section 504 plan, also called the Individual Accommodation Plan (IAP), should be described in the handbook. For example:

▶ *The Individual Accommodation Plan (IAP) will describe the nature of the student's disability and how it substantially affects one or more of the student's major life activities; describe the modifications, accommodations, and/or adaptations determined by the Section 504 Committee to be necessary to provide the student with a free appropriate education; identify the persons responsible for implementing the plan; and identify the criteria to be used in evaluating the success of the plan.*

Discipline

As we pointed out in Chapter 1, discipline of students who are protected under a Section 504 plan requires careful consideration of whether the student's behavior is related to the disabling condition. The handbook should describe the district's policies regarding discipline for Section 504 students. An example follows:

▶ *Prior to the removal of a Section 504 student from her or his current placement for disciplinary reasons, the Section 504 Committee will convene to determine whether the student's behavior is causally related to the handicap. The Committee will consider these factors in its determination: (1) the recommended removal by expulsion or suspension is for an indefinite period of time; (2) the recommended removal by expulsion or suspension is for a period of time in excess of 10[1] consecutive school days during the current school year; (3) the recommended removal by expulsion or suspension is for a period of time which, when added to the student's previous out-of-school suspensions, would total more than 10 school days during the current school year and no reevaluation has been conducted by the Section 504 Committee prior to any of the less-than-10[2]-day suspension periods; or (4) the recommended removal by expulsion or suspension is for any other period of time which constitutes a significant change in placement under Section 504. If the student's behavior is determined to be related to the student's disability, the Section 504 Committee will reevaluate to determine whether the student's current placement is appropriate. If the Section 504 Committee determines that the student's current placement is not appropriate, it will determine the changes in placement necessary to appropriately serve the student in the educational setting.*

---

[1]Note: Some states use a different criterion. In addition, the outcome of current court cases may change this requirement.

[2]See note 1.

Substance Abuse

In Chapter 1 we stated that Section 504 students may not have their placement changed significantly without reevaluation unless the student is engaging in the use or possession of illegal drugs, alcohols, or substances. Regarding this exception, the policy and procedures handbook might contain a statement such as:

▶ *Section 504 students who are recommended for suspension or expulsion solely on the basis of the current use or possession of illegal drugs, alcohol, or substances are not entitled to a Section 504 Committee placement re-evaluation or determination of relationship between such use or possession and the students' disabilities, or to the procedural safeguards afforded to students with a disability by these procedures.*

Parent and Student Rights Under Section 504

Section 504 established certain rights for parents and students. The district handbook should include notice of these to students and their parents/guardians. An example follows:

▶ *Parents/guardians shall be notified in writing of all district decisions concerning the identification, evaluation, or educational placement of their children. Adult students and parents/guardians of minor students shall be provided with notice of their rights under Section 504, including the right to disagree with or appeal the decisions of the Section 504 Committee. These rights include the right to: notice of any proposed action of a Section 504 Committee regarding themselves/their child; examine relevant school records concerning the student; appeal decisions made by the Section 504 Committee; a hearing before an impartial hearing officer in the case of disagreement with any action or proposed action by the Section 504 committee concerning themselves/their child; a review procedure to appeal the decision of an impartial hearing officer.*

Appendix A shows the complete list of the rights described above.

Most districts further specify the procedural safeguards they have approved, including such aspects as parental notice of grievance, preliminary action by the district compliance officer in case of a grievance, acceptance of the district's offer for mediation, the mediation process itself, the impartial due process hearing, the impartial due process hearing review, and complaints to the Office of Civil Rights.

Procedural Safeguards

To ensure that your district is in full compliance with Section 504, the policies and procedures handbook should contain a list of the procedural safeguards, including those regarding parent and student rights under 504. Parents/guardians should be provided their rights under 504:

- when the student is identified as having a potential disability covered under Section 504;

- when eligibility is determined; and
- prior to making any significant change in the accommodation plan for services, including suspension or expulsion.

You will find in Appendix A a sample form for specifying parent/guardian rights.

Summary

In this chapter we have provided an overview of a policies and procedures handbook, including the pertinent components that should be included. As we mentioned at the beginning of the chapter, the scope of this book prevents our offering a comprehensive plan for developing a handbook. Rather, our hope is that we have provided guidance for you in planning your school's or district's efforts toward complying with Section 504.

Developing a
Section 504
Training Program

In our discussion in Chapter 2 of the resources related to implementing Section 504 plans for students, we referred to teacher inservice training sessions as one resource that increases teachers' knowledge about 504 plans as well as their successful implementation of 504 accommodation plans for students. In this chapter we share with you our experiences in designing and conducting Section 504 teacher inservice programs. We include a sample workshop format, supporting overheads, and handouts. These materials can be used as they are or adapted to reflect the needs of your school or community. Whether you intend to offer such inservices yourself, or whether your purpose in reading this book is to learn as much as you can about Section 504, this chapter will provide you with a scheme for organizing and disseminating your knowledge and experiences.

Factors To Consider in Planning a Section 504 Workshop

Who Should Attend

Our experience leads us to advise you to invite teachers, school staff (counselors, school nurse, etc.), community members, and older students and parents to the same workshop rather than to conduct a separate session for parents and community members. In a combined session, everyone hears the same information and has an opportunity to discuss all the pertinent issues in a relatively unemotional setting. We have also found that in a combined session participants can begin to build collaboration and trust, precisely because they are dealing with the same issues at the same time.

What To Include

A session on Section 504 should include several components:

- basic information about the statute and a brief history of its passage and use
- the purpose of Section 504 plans
- a comparison of Section 504 and IDEA
- the components of a Section 504 plan

- practice designing a Section 504 plan
- information about gaining district support for Section 504 plans
- discussion regarding participants' concerns and questions

We provide participants with an agenda and a Section 504 fact sheet, both shown in Appendix B.

The Importance of Tone

Many teachers and school administrators have heard horror stories about Section 504 demands made by parents and child advocates. Consequently, they may approach the workshop with some reticence, even hostility. We have found it crucial to invite everyone to learn about a tool that makes the job of educating students with special needs more relevant, and, in many cases, easier.

We have found that the audience relaxes if we include discussion of optimistic perspectives on students and 504, emphasis on student strengths instead of disorders, and focus on the diversity of the students falling under Section 504. Moreover, we have found that the audience becomes more resistant if we focus on pessimistic views, on the most severe behavioral issues that can arise, or on what's wrong with students. We recommend that you realize that Section 504 offers a means by which we can all do our jobs better, whether we're teachers, administrators, or parents.

In the handout we provide participants in the workshops we conduct, we include the description of strengths we offered in Chapter 1 in the section titled, "Focusing on Student Strengths." We also lead participants through the Reflection Checklist (see Chapter 2). The Reflection Checklist offers a means for you to focus the group's attention on the nature of the school's practices and to emphasize a vision of caring in education. The checklist can serve as the basis for discussions among members of the workshop about their own beliefs and practices and for the basis of understanding Section 504 as a method for improving teaching in general.

The Importance of Participation

The provision of time for participants to work together in small groups practicing writing 504 plans is essential for the workshop to succeed. Without it, participants typically report that they do not thoroughly understand the material presented. You can enlist someone from each small group to act as facilitator to lead the group through the simulation of writing several 504 plans.

Small-Group Makeup

Divide the larger group into small groups of four to six people who have different roles. Mix teachers, parents, administrators, support staff, and community members so that the groups more closely resemble a Section 504 Committee.

Choosing Modifications

Using a Section 504 Plan form (sold by PRO-ED, order number 8647), the participants can practice writing modifications for two or three scenarios, depending on how much time the groups have. We recommend that the groups spend the bulk of their time on the modifications portion of their simulated 504 plans, as this is the most difficult and critical part of the plan. We have provided three scenarios in Appendix B as examples of what you might like to use for this portion of the workshop, or for your use as models for writing your own scenarios.

Discussion

We strongly urge that you plan discussion time for the large gorup after the practice sessions. Many questions and issues arise when the small groups write their sample plans. Because some of the questions are likely to involve legal and practical issues related to 504, you may wish to invite colleagues to assist you who have expertise in these areas so they can address questions during the workshop or during later follow-up.

Agenda

Most of our experience in conducting Section 504 workshops has been with one-day programs. While we would prefer the luxury of a longer period of time to allow participants to achieve a greater depth of understanding of the issues and processes related to Section 504, the reality seems to be that most districts allot only one day. Still, a significant amount can be covered during 6 or 7 hours of concentrated work.

In our workshops we use a combination of teaching strategies: lecture, overhead transparency outlines and figures, small-group activities, and small- and large-group discussions. Appendix B includes a sample agenda for a one-day Section 504 inservice training program.

In the following sections, we describe each component of the agenda and indicate what materials we include in the workshop handout.

Components of a One-Day
Section 504 Inservice

Overview and History of Section 504

In this introductory portion of the workshop, we typically provide a brief overview of Section 504. Following the outline of our comments in Chapter 1, we describe the history of the statute and its relationship to the Rehabilitation Act of 1973. We emphasize that 504 is an antidiscrimination law that has recently moved to the forefront of attention in education as a result of the activities of advocates interested in securing rights for themselves and their children.

In our handout we include a description of the statute itself to generate discussion about what constitutes a "handicap" and what the statute means by "is regarded as having a handicap." To understand fully how to consider the referral and eligibility of students under Section 504, the workshop participants must understand these issues.

Comparison with IDEA

Workshop participants must be able to differentiate between Section 504 and IDEA in order to take advantage of what both offer. Included in our workshop handout is the IDEA/504 Flow Chart shown in Chapter 1, Figure 1.1, which compares 504 with IDEA. This flow chart provides a visual schema that indicates the critical differences between the two laws, as well as the similarities and overlaps. As you can see from examining Figure 1.1, the emphasis is on the provision of a free appropriate public education (FAPE) based on student need.

At this point during the workshop, we ask participants to complete the Reflection Checklist, described and shown in Chapter 2. Because we emphasize that Section 504 provides a means for becoming better teachers and for designing better instruction for students, the Reflection Checklist serves as a discussion tool around these concepts. From the Reflection Checklist discussion we segue into the Section 504 process, topics we covered in Chapter 2. We lead the participants through a consideration of factors to consider before the 504 plan is developed, such as when to consider a 504 plan and what it might accomplish for a student, what constitutes the 504 evaluation, developing a 504 modification plan, implementing the plan, evaluating the effectiveness of the plan, and modifying the plan based on the evaluation.

Purpose of a Section 504 Plan

Workshop participants need to know that the primary purpose of Section 504 is to prevent discrimination against persons with disabilities. Also, we use the workshop to share our view of the 504 plan as a tool for improving our own teaching and our students' experiences of school and learning. We often spend time with participants discussing how our attitudes toward and views of diversity, inclusion, disability, and disorder (among others) influence our perceptions of students' abilities and potential.

During this portion of the workshop we share with the participants the "What Are Strengths?" sheet (included in their handout) based on our discussion in Chapter 1 on student strengths. An adaptation of "What Are Strengths?" (Salleeby, 1997) is included in Chapter 1. We ask the participants to reflect on their own strengths and to begin the practice of describing themselves and their children/students in terms of strengths. We discuss the effects of labeling students with disorder terms and the common practice of confusing the student with the label, saying such things as "He's learning disabled" rather than "He has a learning disability."

Components of a Section 504 Plan

Our workshop handout contains a copy of the list entitled "Components of a 504 Plan" (see Chapter 2) to give participants an overview of what is essential to include on a student's plan. This sheet is *not* an example of an actual plan. Rather, it is intended to provide a visual picture of what each plan should include. It is important to remember that different states and districts may have more specific requirements regarding the core components. Our handout sheet shows only the basics required by the federal statute.

We use this sheet to guide a general discussion of referral, parent notification, evaluation and determination of eligibility, design of reasonable accommodations, criteria to be used to measure the accomplishment of the plan, and setting of a review/reassessment date. When the participants break out into small groups later in the workshop, they likely will return to some of these issues in their efforts to write 504 plans based on the scenarios we provide.

Small Groups Writing Simulated 504 Plans

The small-group breakout sessions provide the meat of the workshop, as the participants experience the actual design of a 504 accommodation plan, using the scenarios contained in their handout. The handout also includes a "Sample Section 504 Referral Documentation Form" and a "Sample Section 504 Evaluation Documentation Form"; we want the workshop participants to practice using a "real-life" format when developing their simulated plans.

In the workshops we conduct, we provide a significant amount of time for these small groups to practice writing 504 plans (see the agenda in Appendix B for specific details regarding time allotted for this process). As facilitators we act as consultants for each of the small groups, answering questions and providing information as needed. In addition, we provide participants with another handout sheet describing a positive process for designing and implementing Section 504 modification plans (See Appendix B). The process described in this handout organizes the 504 process so that participants can see how to plan during three phases of the 504 planning process: (1) before the 504 plan is actually developed, (2) during the 504 process, and (3) after the plan has been developed, while it is being implemented. This organizational planner acts as a reminder for participants, some of whom translate it into a checklist to ensure that they have addressed the many aspects of the 504 planning process.

Before the small groups begin their actual plan writing, we take them through a discussion about how to think about modifications, using the sheet titled, "Thinking About Modifications," included in Appendix B. Based on our own learning about designing 504 modifications, we have found that the seven guidelines shown in the handout ease the process considerably because they serve to forestall problems that can arise when one is just beginning to learn about the 504 process. As we circulate through the small groups as they write their plans, we refer them to this sheet as a way of checking the accommodations they are recommending for the scenarios.

Large-Group Discussion

As important as the small-group breakout sessions are, participants value the time spent with the larger group discussing their experiences during the breakouts. During this large-group discussion, participants typically raise issues related to a range of topics, including concern about their own district or school, their desire to improve their abilities as teachers, or their concern about students for whom they are interested in finding assistance.

The large-group discussion also frequently focuses on the creativity the small groups used in designing 504 plans for the scenarios. While there is overlap between groups' ideas, the differences expressed during the large-group discussion serve to enrich everyone's experience of the plan-writing process.

Planning for District Support

We frequently hear from participants that their districts are resistant to voluntarily providing Section 504 plans, to making modifications in instruction for students who do not qualify for special education services under IDEA, or to the idea that all students can benefit from the accommodations that arise as a consequence of the 504 plans written for a few students.

Summary

In this chapter we have shared with you our ideas about how to organize and conduct a workshop on Section 504 for teachers, administrators, parents, students, and community members. We described the factors to consider when planning such a workshop and the components to be included in the workshop. We have referred you to previous chapters as well as the appendixes to point out various handout materials we recommend using during the workshop.

Sample Forms for a Policies and Procedures Handbook

Sample Notice to Parent(s)/Guardian(s) of Section 504 Evaluation and Committee Meeting

Date _____

To Parent(s)/Guardian(s) of _____ Birthdate _____

School _____ Grade _____

The student named above has been referred to the school district as possibly being eligible under Section 504 as having a disabling condition.

This letter is to provide you with written notice that, to determine whether your child is eligible, an evaluation will be conducted at a Section 504 Committee Meeting. Your attendance at this meeting is welcomed, but it is not required by law.

Date of Meeting _____ Time _____

Location _____

    If your child is determined to be eligible under Section 504, the Committee will develop an accommodation plan to address your child's educational needs and make an appropriate placement.

    For your further information, we have included a description of Section 504 and the rights you and your child are entitled to under Section 504 of the Rehabilitation Act of 1973. Please sign and return the attached form to verify that you have received your notification of your parent and student rights and to confirm your attendance at the scheduled Section 504 Evaluation Meeting.

    If you have any questions or need additional information, please address your questions to:

Section 504 School Designee _____

Telephone Number _____

© 1998 by PRO-ED, Inc.

Sample Acknowledgment of Receipt of Notice of Section 504 Evaluation and Committee Meeting

To: Section 504 School Designee _____:

By my signature below, I verify that I have received:

the "Notice to Parents of Section 504 Evaluation and Committee Meeting" and
the "Parent/Student Rights in Identification, Evaluation, and Placement under Section 504."

Regarding the Section 504 Evaluation and Committee Meeting that has been scheduled for my child:

(Please check the appropriate boxes below)

[   ]   I intend to be there. Do not conduct the meeting in my absence.

[   ]   I intend to be there. However, you may proceed without me if I am unable to attend. Please forward to me a copy of the completed Section 504 Evaluation form for my review and signature.

[   ]   I will not attend. Please forward to me a copy of the completed Section 504 Evaluation form for my review and signature.

[   ]   Please provide an interpreter for the Section 504 Evaluation and Committee meeting that has been scheduled.

_____

(Please specify language, include signing.)

Signed_____   Phone _____/_____
                                                     (Home)   (Work)

Date_____

> Please read, sign, and return this form as soon as possible to:
> Section 504 School Designee
>
> _____
>
> _____

© 1998 by PRO-ED, Inc.

Sample Information Regarding Section 504 of the Rehabilitation Act of 1973

Section 504 is an Act prohibiting discrimination against anyone with a handicap in any program receiving federal financial assistance. The Act defines a person with a handicap as anyone who:

1. has a mental or physical impairment which substantially limits one or more major life activities, including activities such as caring for oneself, performing manual tasks, walking, seeing, hearing, speaking, breathing, learning, and working;

2. has a record of such an impairment; or

3. is regarded as having such an impairment.

In order to fulfill its obligation under Section 504, the _____ school district recognizes a responsibility to avoid discrimination in policies and practices regarding its personnel and students. No discrimination against any person with a handicap will knowingly be permitted in any of the programs and practices of the school system.

The school district has specific responsibilities under the Act, which include the responsibility to identify, evaluate, and, if the child is determined to be eligible under Section 504, afford access to educational services.

If the parent or guardian disagrees with the determination made by the professional staff of the school district, she or he has a right to a hearing with an impartial hearing officer.

The Family Educational Rights and Privacy Act (FERPA) also specifies rights related to educational records. This Act gives the parent or guardian the right to: (1) inspect and review her/his child's educational records; (2) make copies of these records; (3) receive a list of all individuals having access to those records; (4) ask for an explanation of any item in the records; (5) ask for an amendment to any report on the grounds that it is inaccurate, misleading, or violates the child's rights; and (6) a hearing on the issue if the school refuses to make the amendment.

If you have questions, please feel free to contact _____, the Section 504 Coordinator for the school district, at phone number _____.

© 1998 by PRO-ED, Inc.

Sample Notice of Parent/Student Rights in Identification, Evaluation, and Placement Under Section 504

The following is a description of the rights granted by federal law, Section 504 of the Rehabilitation Act of 1973, to students with disabilities. The intent of the law is to keep you fully informed concerning decisions about your child as well as to inform you of your rights if you disagree with any of these decisions.
You have the right to:

1. have your child take part in, and benefit from, public education programs without discrimination because of her or his disabling conditions;

2. have the school district advise you of your rights under federal law;

3. receive notice regarding identification, evaluation, placement, or change of placement of your child;

4. receive information in your native language and primary mode of communication;

5. have your child receive a free appropriate public education. This includes the right to be educated with students without disabilities to the maximum extent appropriate. It also includes the right to have the school district make reasonable accommodations to allow your chlild an equal opportunity to participate in school and school-related activities.

6. have your child educated in facilities and receive services comparable to those provided to students without disabilities;

7. have your child receive special education and/or related services if he or she is found to be eligible under the Individuals with Disabilities Act (P.L. 101-476) or Section 504 of the Rehabilitation Act;

8. have evaluation, educational, and placement decisions made based upon a variety of information sources and by persons who know the student, the evaluation data, and placement options;

9. have periodic reevaluations and an evaluation prior to any significant change in program or service modifications, including placement;

10. have transportation provided to and from an alternative placement setting at no greater cost to you than would be incurred if the student were placed in a program operated by the district;

11. have your child be given an equal opportunity to participate in nonacademic and extracurricular activities offered by the district;

12. examine all relevant records relating to decisions regarding your child's identification, evaluation, educational program, and placement;

13. obtain copies of educational records at a reasonable cost unless the fee would effectively deny you access to the records;

© 1998 by PRO-ED, Inc.

14. a response from the school district to reasonable requests for explanations and interpretations of your child's records;

15. request amendment of your child's educational records if there is reasonable cause to believe that they are inaccurate, misleading, or otherwise in violation of the privacy rights of your child. If the school district refuses this request for amendment, it shall notify you within a reasonable time and advise you of your right to a hearing;

16. request mediation or an impartial due-process hearing related to decisions or actions regarding your child's identification, evaluation, educational program, or placement (you and the student may take part in the hearing and have an attorney represent you; hearing requests must be made to _____);

17. ask for payment of reasonable attorney fees if you are successful on your claim; and

18. file a local grievance.

The person in this district who is responsible for assuring that the district complies with Section 504 is _____ (telephone number _____).

© 1998 by PRO-ED, Inc.

Sample Handouts for a Section 504 Workshop

Sample 504 Scenarios

Scenario #1

Ms. Smith has a physician's statement indicating that her son Chris has Attention Deficit Disorder. Chris has started on a trial of Ritalin, which he takes twice a day. Chris's third-grade teacher and his second-grade teacher from last year both express concerns about Chris's inability to stay focused on school work, especially when he is required to complete written work on his own. He gets started right away, but he soon wanders away or begins to talk to others about unrelated topics. He asks for teacher guidance frequently, sometimes every 3 or 4 minutes. They also report that Chris gets along well with others and is well liked by adults and peers. Chris was evaluated by his school in second grade and found not eligible for special education services. His reading and math skills are both at grade level. He is not a behavior problem, other than the fact that his being off-task so much distracts other students. Since Chris has started on medication, he is completing more work and his handwriting has improved, but his teacher reports that he still appears to tire quickly when completing written work and that he still has difficulty following multistep directions. Ms. Smith and the Section 504 Committee will work together to develop a 504 plan for Chris.

Scenario #2

Mark is a ninth grader who broke his leg and will be on crutches approximately 7 weeks. His parents are concerned that several of his teachers are penalizing him for being late to class. While they do not mark him late, they often give assignments or collect homework immediately after the bell rings (before Mark gets there). When Mark's mother talked with the teachers, they shared that Mark was sometimes late for class before he broke his leg and that he talks and "cuts up" in class. They say all he has to do is ask another student for the assignment and remember to turn his homework in on his own. They feel he is old enough to take responsibility for this himself and that

© 1998 by PRO-ED, Inc.

Mom is being overly protective. The assistant principal offers to convene a Section 504 committee to address these concerns.

Scenario #3

Lisa is a fifth grader with diabetes. Her parents have furnished documentation of her condition and of her need to have access during the day to equipment to test her blood sugar level for herself. She also needs insulin administered at times during the school day. There is a school nurse at Lisa's school one day a week.

© 1998 by PRO-ED, Inc.

Fact Sheet: Section 504 of the Rehabilitation Act

What Is Section 504?

No otherwise qualified individual with handicaps in the United States shall, solely by reason of her or his handicap, as defined in section 706(8) of this title, be excluded from the participation in, be denied the benefits of, or be subjected to discrimination under any program or activity receiving Federal financial assistance or under any program or activity conducted by any Executive agency or by the United States Postal Service. (29 U.S.C. Sec. 794)

The act provides a set of definitions that explicate exactly what is meant by *individual with a handicap* and defines the impact of the handicap or condition on a *major life activity*. Thus, *individual with handicaps* is defined as:

any individual who

(i)   has a physical or mental impairment which substantially limits one or more of such person's major life activities,

(ii) has a record of such impairment, or

(iii) is regarded as having such an impairment. (29 U.S.C. Sec. 706.(8))

Further, *physical or mental impairment* is described as:

(A) any physiological disorder or condition, cosmetic disfigurement, or anatomical loss affecting one or more of the following body systems: neurological; musculoskeletal; special sense organs; respiratory, including speech organs; cardiovascular; reproductive; digestive; genito-urinary; hermic and lymphatic; skin; and endocrine; or

(B) any mental or psychological disorder, such as mental retardation, organic brain syndrome, emotional or mental illness, and specific learning disabilities. (34 Code of Federal Regulations Part 104.3)

Major life activities are defined as:

functions such as caring for one's self, performing manual tasks, walking, seeing, hearing, speaking, breathing, learnihng and working. (34 Code of Federal Regulations Part 104.3)

Has a record of such an impairment means:

has a history of, or has been classified as having, a mental or physical impairment that substantially limits one or more major life activities. (34 Code of Federal Regulations Part 104.3)

© 1998 by PRO-ED, Inc.

Is regarded as having an impairment is defined as:

(A) has a physical or mental impairment that does not substantially limit major life activities but is treated by a recipient as constituting such a limitation;

(B) has a physical or mental impairment that substantially limits major life activities only as a result of the attitudes of others toward such impairment; or

(C) has none of the impairments defined but is treated by a recipient as having such an impairment. (34 Code of Federal Regulations Part 104.3)

General Purpose

Section 504 is a broad civil rights law that protects the rights of individuals with disabilities in programs and activities that receive federal financial assistance from the U.S. Department of Education.

Who Is Protected?

Section 504 protects all school-age children who qualify as disabled, in other words, who (1) have or (2) have had a physical or mental impairment which substantially limits a major life activity, or (3) are regarded as disabled by others. Major life activities include walking, seeing, breathing, learning, working, caring for oneself, and performing manual tasks. The disabling condition need only limit one major life activity in order for the student to be eligible. Children who are receiving special education services under the Individuals with Disabilities Act (IDEA) are also protected by Section 504.

Examples of potential 504 disabling conditions *not* typically covered under IDEA are:

- communicable diseases;
- tuberculosis;
- HIV/AIDS;
- medical condition (asthma, allergies, diabetes, heart disease);
- temporary conditions due to illness or accident;
- Attention-Deficit/Hyperactivity Disorder;
- behavioral difficulties; and
- drug/alcohol addiction (if the student is no longer using drugs/alcohol).

What a 504 Plan Provides

- An evaluation based on current levels of performance, teacher reports, and documentation of areas of concern

© 1998 by PRO-ED, Inc.

- The development/implementation of an accommodation plan that specifies "reasonable" modifications in order for the student to benefit from her or his educational program

- Procedural safeguards for students and parents, including written notification of all district decisions concerning the student's evaluation or educational placement and due process

- Review and reevaluation of modifications and placement on a regular basis and prior to any significant change in placement

When to Consider a 504 Plan

- A student shows a pattern of not benefitting from the instruction being provided.

- Retention is being considered.

- A student returns to school after a serious illness or injury.

- Long-term suspension or expulsion is being considered.

- A student is evaluated and found not eligible for special education services or is transitioning out of special education.

- A student exhibits a chronic health or mental health condition.

- Substance abuse is an issue.

- A student is "at risk" for dropping out.

- A student is taking medication at school.

© 1998 by PRO-ED, Inc.

Sample Agenda for a One-Day Section 504 Inservice Program

9:00 a.m.–9:50 a.m.   Overview of Section 504

Why 504? Why Now?

> The Rehabilitation Act of 1973, P.L. 94-142, P.L. 101-476 (IDEA)

> Inclusion, increase in students ineligible for IDEA, special education outcomes research

> Why 504 is "right" for our times

Purpose of 504 Plans

> Section 504 Fact Sheet

>> Definitions

>> What Section 504 provides

>> When a 504 plan should be considered

Philosophy and Comparison with IDEA

> IDEA/504 Flow Chart[a]

> A Reflection Checklist for your school[b]

> The Section 504 process

9:50 a.m.–10:00 a.m.   Break

10:00 a.m.–11:00 a.m.   Components of a Section 504 Plan

> Referral information and source

> Referral review and parent notification

> Eligibility determination

> Evaluation: Present levels of performance (strengths and needs)

>> Parent information and concerns

>> Teacher reports/comments

>> Areas of concern

---

[a]This is the chart we showed in Chapter 1 as Figure 1.1.

[b]We showed the Reflection Checklist in Chapter 2.

© 1998 by PRO-ED, Inc.

	Health and development history
	Reasonable accommodations
	Criteria for measuring accomplishment of plan
	Review/Reassessment date
	Signatures of participants
11:00 a.m.–12:00 p.m.	Step-by-Step through the Process: Small-group practice breakouts and large-group sharing
12:00 p.m.–1:00 p.m.	Lunch
1:00 p.m.–2:30 p.m.	Step-by-Step Through the Process: Small-group practice breakouts and large-group discussion, continued
2:30 p.m.–3:30 p.m.	Developing District Support
	How to disseminate in your district
	How to overcome resistance
	Appropriate collaboration strategies
3:30 p.m.–4:00 p.m.	Questions/Responses/Discussion

© 1998 by PRO-ED, Inc.

A Positive Process for Designing and Implementing Section 504 Modification Plans

In the Preparatory Phase

1. Identify a Section 504 compliance officer for the district.

2. Identify and train a designated 504 facilitator for each school. Typically, this person is a teacher or administrator already on staff; sometimes this person is a community volunteer.

3. Identify and designate specific resources and support for teachers who will be implementing Section 504 plans in their classrooms. Examples of resources and support for teachers might include a districtwide consultant on Section 504; the establishment of common planning or preparation times for teachers to meet to discuss issues related to Section 504 plans; the development of a handbook containing district policies and procedures regarding Section 504; examples of 504 plans from other districts; examples of modifications and accommodations related to specific types of disabilities; information regarding disabling conditions; scheduled meetings for teachers with the district Section 504 facilitator to provide information and answer questions.

Once Section 504 Procedures Are in Place

1. Give appropriate and timely notification to parents/families about the intent to develop a Section 504 plan.

2. Schedule continued meetings for teachers with the district Section 504 facilitator to discuss which strategies/modifications best support student success, with focus on the least intrusive modifications needed.

3. Make the district Section 504 facilitator available to meet with parents/families and the student—*prior* to the 504 meeting—to help identify the student's strengths and needs as well as everyone's concerns.

4. Schedule enough time for the 504 meeting so that a relaxed and positive discussion can take place and so that everyone can agree on modifications that are reasonable and achievable.

5. Focus the meeting on the goal of student success and self-management.

6. Set a review schedule to ensure that the plan is working.

After the 504 Plan Is Initiated

1. Continue to provide teachers with access to support and/or feedback about the modifications that are being implemented.

© 1998 by PRO-ED, Inc.

2. Continue scheduled communication between parents and staff about questions, successes, and ongoing effectiveness of the plan.

3. Review and, if necessary, modify the plan yearly to accommodate maturation and learning as well as different teaching styles and schedules.

© 1998 by PRO-ED, Inc.

Thinking About Modifications

Perhaps the most important component of the Section 504 plan is the description of the modifications planned to increase the opportunity of success for the student. Teachers, the student (when appropriate), parent/guardian, and administrators can work together on the Section 504 Committee to identify and describe the modifications to be implemented. Some general guidelines for planning modifications include:

1. *Focus on the student's strengths.* Begin every modification plan with a focus on the student's strengths. Ask what is going well and how we can build on the student's existing success. Find out the student's interests: What does the student seek out? How might problem areas inform us about what this student needs? Then, how can we build on assets in this situation to help this student have her or his needs met?

2. *Design the least intrusive intervention.* Modifications should be designed to be as close to the general classroom procedures and methods as possible. For instance, rather than changing the student's math work by giving a different assignment, specify instead that the student will do every other problem.

3. *Customize the modifications to fit the student's classroom setup.* Modifications should be designed so that teachers can implement in a way that makes sense for their program. For instance, specify allowing a reasonable amount of extra time for assignments to be turned in, rather than saying that work can be turned in two days late. As far as possible, customize the modification to the learner, the classroom, the assignment, the curriculum, and the teacher's teaching methods.

4. *Consider academic modifications first.* Even when the student's behavior seems to be the major issue, consider whether modifying his or her academic workload may reduce the student's belief that the demands are overwhelming. When adjustments in expectations are made, behavior issues may diminish or disappear completely.

5. *Match the modifications to the student's strengths and needs.* Choose only those modifications that are needed, attending to what the student needs and what is most likely to work given this student's strengths. Don't fix what isn't broken.

6. *Prioritize and implement only a few modifications at a time.* In our experience, specifying multiple changes at one time overwhelms everyone—teacher(s), parent(s), and student. Pick two or three modifications to begin with, and use follow-up team meetings to make adjustments as needed. This procedure also helps the team determine which modifications are effective and which are not.

7. *Review and adjust accommodations continuously.* Because the 504 plan is the beginning of the process, take the position that reviewing and adjusting are requisite parts of the process. Engage in the 504 process as an ongoing endeavor that works best with continual reviewing and modifying. Schedule appropriate intervals for reviewing the plan.

© 1998 by PRO-ED, Inc.

Glossary[1]

Adaptive Behavior The effectiveness with which a student meets the standards of personal independence and social responsibility expected of her or his age and cultural group. (34 CFR 104.35 c [1])

Adult Student For school purposes, a student 18 or more years of age; considered a legal adult unless a court has declared the student incompetent. The adult student assumes all the rights of parents described in this publication. The school must treat the student as an adult. However, continued participaton of parents, with student permission, is encouraged.

Code of Federal Regulations (CFR) The published rules of the federal government which all agencies and facilities receiving federal financial assistance are required to follow.

Disabled (According to Section 504) having a physical or mental impairment that substantially limits one or more major life activity, having a record of such an impairment, or regarded as having such an impairment.

Due Process Rights Parent(s)'/guardian(s)' right to an impartial hearing, with an opportunity to participate and to be represented by counsel, in the event of a disagreement between the parent(s)/guardian(s) and the district in regard to the identification, evaluation, or educational services of a student with a disability.

Eligibility A student's right to services under Section 504 if she or he has, has a record of having, or is regarded as having a physical or mental impairment that substantially limits a major life activity.

Educational Setting The entire school environment, both inside and outside the school building, including but not limited to the gymnasium, cafeteria, auditorium, playground, classrooms inside the school building, portable classrooms, physical structure of the school, and any curricular activities, such as field trips.

Evaluation An inquiry conducted to determine whether a student has a disability under Section 504. Evaluation data may include, but are not limited to, formal and informal test instruments, aptitude and achievement tests, teacher recommendations, physical or medical records, student grades, progress reports, parent observations, and anecdotal records. An evaluation must also be conducted before any significant changes in placement in the instructional program (e.g., alternative education programs, suspensions, or expulsions).

IDEA (the Individuals with Disabilities Education Act) A federal funding statute passed by Congress to provide financial aid to states in their efforts to ensure adequate and appropriate services to children with disabilities.

Impairment (1) Any physiological disorder or condition, cosmetic disfigurement, or anatomical loss affecting one or more of the following body systems: neurological; musculoskeletal; special sense

---

[1]Adapted with permission from Livovich (1995).

organs; respiratory, including speech organs; cardiovascular; digestive; hemic and lymphatic; skin; and endocrine; (2) any mental or psychological disorder, organic brain syndrome, emotional or mental illness, and specific learning disabilities.

Individual Accommodation Plan (IAP) A document developed by the school's Section 504 Committee that determines a student's eligibility, specific modifications in the educational environment, and supportive services deemed appropriate for the student to receive a free appropriate public education.

Major Life Activity Functions such as walking, seeing, hearing, speaking, breathing, learning, working, caring for oneself, and performing manual tasks.

Mediation The process used to resolve disagreements between parents/guardians and the Section 504 Committee regarding decisions the Committee has made regarding their child. During mediation, the parents/guardians voluntarily meet with a school representative and a mediator (an impartial third party) to review the student's plan and to work out solutions satisfactory to all parties.

Nondiscrimination The guarantee, under federal law, that no qualified disabled person, shall, on the basis of the disability, be excluded from participation in, be denied the benefits of, or otherwise be subjected to discrimination under any program or activity that receives or benefits from federal financial assistance.

Notice Prior written information provided by the school to the parents/guardians about the actions or proposed actions regarding Section 504 for their child. Whenever possible, this notice will be in the parents'/guardians' native language. If this is not possible, the school must use other means to ensure that the parents/guardians understand the information in the notice.

Reevaluation A review of eligibility and the need for Section 504 services, which must occur at least every three years for as long as the student is receiving services under the protection of Section 504. The reevaluation will follow the same guidelines as the original evaluation. Reevaluation may be done more often if conditions warrant, such as a significant change in student placement.

Section 504 A federal law, part of the Rehabilitation Act passed in 1973. It is designed to eliminate discrimination on the basis of a disability in any program or activity receiving federal financial assistance. Section 504 disabilities include any physical or mental impairment which substantially limits one or more of a person's major life activities.

Special Education Instruction and related services provided to students who have met the criteria for one or more of the 13 categories under the Individuals with Disabilities Education Act (IDEA).

References

Council of Administrators of Special Education. (1992). *Student access: A resource guide for educators: Section 504 of the Rehabilitation Act of 1973.* Reston, VA: Council for Exceptional Children.

Doudy, C. A., Patton, J. R., Smith, T. C., & Polloway, E. A. (1997). *Attention-Deficit/Hyperactivity Disorder in the classroom.* Austin, TX: PRO-ED.

Education for All Handicapped Children Act of 1975, 20 U.S.C. § 1400 *et seq.*

Family Educational Rights and Privacy Act of 1974, 20 U.S.C. § 1232 *et seq.*

Gallup–McKinley County School District. (1996). *Section 504 Handbook.* Gallup, NM: Gallup–McKinley County School District.

Gardner, H. A. (1993). *Multiple intelligences: Theory into practice.* New York: Basic Books.

Gibbs, J. (1994). *Tribes: A new way of learning together.* Santa Rosa, CA: Center Source Publications.

Hoover, J. J., & Patton, J. R. (1997). *Curriculum adaptations for students with learning and behavior problems: Principles and practices* (2nd ed.). Austin, TX: PRO-ED.

Individuals with Disabilities Education Act of 1990, 20 U.S.C. § 1400 *et seq.*

Johnson , D. W., & Johnson, R. T. (1990). Mainstreaming and cooperative learning strategies. *Exceptional Children, 52,* 553–561.

Livovich, M. P., Jr. (1995). *Section 504 of the Rehabilitation Act of 1973 and the Americans with Disabilities Act: Providing access to a free appropriate education: A principal's manual.* Chesterton, IN: ACCESS.

Miller, L. (1991). *The Smart Profile: A qualitative approach for describing learners and designing instruction.* Austin, TX: Smart Alternatives.

Miller, L. (1992). *Your Personal Smart Profile: A qualitative approach for describing yourself in your everyday life.* Austin, TX: Smart Alternatives.

Miller, L. (1993a). Testing and the creation of disorder. *American Journal of Speech–Language Pathology, 2,* 13–16.

Miller, L. (1993b). *What we call smart: A new narrative for intelligence and learning.* San Diego: Singular.

Miller, L., & Miller, L. C. (1994). *The Quick Smart Profile.* Austin, TX: Smart Alternatives.

Miller, L., & Miller, L. C. (1996). *The Quick Smart Profile for Kids.* Austin, TX: Smart Alternatives.

Miller, L., & Newbill, C. (1992). Innovative instructional programs for students with learning and/or behavioral disorders. *Clinics in Communication Disorders, 2,* 2, 19–31.

Newbill, C. M. (1997). Workshop notes.

Polloway, E. A., & Patton, J. R. (1997). *Strategies for teaching learners with special needs* (5th ed.). Columbus, OH: Merrill/Prentice-Hall.

Rehabilitation Act of 1973, 29 U.S.C. § 701 *et seq.*

Salleeby, D. (1997). *What are strengths?* Personal communication.

Scruggs, T. E., & Mastropieri, M. A. (1994). Successful mainstreaming in elementary science classes: A qualitative study of three reputable cases. *American Educational Research Journal, 31,* 785–811.

Section 504 Compliance: Issues, Analysis & Cases. (1997). Horsham, PA: LRP Publications.

Smith, D., & Luckesson, R. (1995). *Special education: Teaching in an age of challenge.* New York: Allyn and Bacon.

Smith, T. C., & Patton, J. R. (1998). *Section 504 and public schools: A resource guide for determining eligibility and developing accommodation plans*. Austin, TX: PRO-ED.

Street, S., & Smith, T. E. C. (1996). *Section 504 and public schools: A practical guide*. Little Rock, AR: The Learning Group.

Wood, J. W. (1992). *Adapting instruction for mainstreamed and at-risk students* (2nd ed.). New York: Macmillan.